HOLINESS IN ACTION

IS VOLUME

98

OF THE

Twentieth Century Encyclopedia of Catholicism

UNDER SECTION

IX

THE CHURCH AND THE MODERN WORLD

IT IS ALSO THE

104TH

VOLUME IN ORDER OF PUBLICATION

Edited by HENRI DANIEL-ROPS of the Académie Française

HOLINESS IN ACTION

By ROLAND CLUNY

Preface by Henri Daniel-Rops

Translated from the French by D. A. ASKEW

HAWTHORN BOOKS · PUBLISHERS · *New York*

First Edition, April, 1963

NIHIL OBSTAT

Daniel Duivesteijn, S.T.D.

   Censor Deputatus

IMPRIMATUR

Georgius L. Craven

   Episcopus Sebastopolis, Vic. Cap.

Westmonasterii, die II FEBRUARII MCMLXIII

H-9539

CONTENTS

HOLINESS IN HISTORY AND HOLINESS TODAY

Do you remember that strange passage at the beginning of Claudel's *The Satin Slipper*? For many people in the audience it is something extraneous; they find difficulty in seeing its point. In the prologue to a play about love what is that Jesuit Father doing dying, tied to the mast of a poor Spanish ship, out in the Atlantic, a few degrees below the equator, halfway between the Old World and the New? Look at him, with his torn cassock and his face already marked by his death agony, among "those great splashes of blood, those corpses lying everywhere, those groups of nuns flung down on top of each other". What does it all mean? And what connection does it have with Rodrigo and Prouhèze, face to face with their passion as they might be with a wild animal which they have to overcome if they are not to be devoured by it?

What connection does it have? The answer is the closest of connections. I myself once heard Claudel say: "The most important thing in *The Satin Slipper* is the prologue." And then, with that harsh, but very youthful laugh that was his right up to his death, he quoted to me the ironical little sentence which the announcer throws out to the public, who laugh at it, too, but without understanding what it really means: "It's what you won't understand that is the finest." And it is precisely what the public does not understand that gives the play its real meaning, and establishes its dimensions.

If Rodrigo and Prouhèze finally overcome their adulterous passion, in spite of the terrible temptation to which they are prey, it is because God gives them the grace. And why does he give them the grace? Because out there, in the middle of the Atlantic, on a disabled old hulk, their brother the Jesuit died asking God for it—because, as the poet says, he "translated in heaven" what they "pitifully attempted to say on earth".

But there is more: in Claudel's symbolism, the cosmic tragedy is superimposed on the psychological tragedy. By contrast with Prouhèze, who represents faith, Rodrigo is the type of the new man—exalted by the will for power and fascinated by the desire to possess the world, and imagining that he has been freed of God. The drama lies between these two forces, and it is in this drama that the martyr intervenes on a supernatural level. It is because he dies, as St Francis Xavier died at the gates of China, and as many others have died, that the Church of Christ was to emerge from the crisis in which the world saw her to be immersed; it is because of his merits, mysteriously poured out on the whole of mankind, that heresy was not to triumph, that there was to be a Council and a Counter-Reformation, and that we witness that missionary expansion by which the losses inflicted on Catholicism were made up, and more than made up.

At the end of the conversation which I have already mentioned, in which Claudel spoke to me at length about *The Satin Slipper*, the old poet added, in a softer voice and with an air of unshakeable conviction: "Perhaps, in the end, the sinking boat also represents our own world, battered and shaken by all the storms of apostasy and madness, but protected, in spite of everything, by priests, like that poor Jesuit tied to his broken mast, who are dying for the faith in China and elsewhere. . . ."

Thus, in the poet's vision, the prayer of the dying Jesuit was not offered just for Rodrigo and Prouhèze, but for the whole of mankind, that is, for each of us.

History produces a whole host of proofs which confirm the truth intuitively proclaimed, in an unforgettable image, by this Christian poet. When a Church historian whom I know is asked what seems to him to be the most extraordinary and the most significant element in these past twenty centuries, during which, despite devastating hurricanes and earthquakes, we have seen the grain of seed planted on the hills of Galilee grow up into the immense tree which now confronts us, he can only reply that the most important and the most significant element is the history of holiness; or, better, that the real history of the Church is the history of holiness.

It is undoubtedly extremely interesting to know the political history of the Church—the history of her insertion into the world, and of her struggles with the powers of the world; undoubtedly, too, it would be impossible to write the history of the Church without paying some attention to the history of her thought, to the development of her dogma and to those other struggles which she has carried on in order to defend the sacred deposit entrusted to her. But if her history were to be limited to these two chapters, it would simply be the history of a political party and of a philosophical school—and we know perfectly well that the Church is neither a political party nor a philosophical school. It is precisely because she is much more than either that her real leaders are not the politicians nor the thinkers —and not even, I dare to say, the theologians—but often those obscure, sacrificial witnesses who, like Claudel's Jesuit, offer their lives in order to take all the values and

all the dramas of their age upon themselves, and, we repeat
with the poet, "translate them in heaven".

One of the most striking and, I must add, one of the
most mysterious facts in the history of the Church is that
men and women like this, invested with this sort of mission,
can be found in all places and at all periods; they have
never been lacking. We might even feel impelled to say that
there is an unformulated, but absolute law which decrees
that sanctity should spring up exactly where it is needed
and in the form in which it can be most effective. Christ's
promise to us when he was returning to the Father: "I
am with you until the consummation of the world", is
fulfilled in his saints. Can we imagine what the history of
our civilization would be like if we eliminated from it all
those saints whose names are familiar to us, to say nothing
of the numberless host of what Péguy used to call the
piétaille, of those whom we have forgotten, but who have
all helped to make the Kingdom grow? Such a history is,
in fact, quite inconceivable, or, better, it simply could not
be.

In the dialectic of history, holiness seems to play a
double rôle. On the one hand, the saints, far from cutting
themselves off from the world and turning their backs on
their own times, as idle people like to think, have an
exceptional knowledge and a heartbreaking awareness of
their own age, of the society in which they live, and of its
spiritual needs and failings—in a word, of its sins. Thus,
the Jesuit in *The Satin Slipper* knows, all through his aching
flesh, what are the sins for which he is atoning by his
death. In this way, the saints come to us as the *judges* of
their own period and society.

But, since, by their example, their words and sometimes
only by their prayers, they also witness to the truth which
is the way and the life, they are set up as *guides* for the

men among whom it is given to them to live. There is no saint who has not served in this double capacity. And how many, among the very greatest of them, have been prodigiously successful in this double rôle!

It is obvious that, in the short space which has been allotted to me, I cannot hope to follow the course of Christian history in order to show how this sort of law applies. At the most, a few examples might be selected to illustrate my thesis.

Scarcely had the Church been born, when she was already threatened by a danger—by the secret temptation to exclusiveness, to a certain formalism, and even to a narrow, national traditionalism. If she had given way to it her destiny would have been blocked for ever—she would never have been anything more than a tiny Jewish sect, a sort of popular Essenism. But a man arose—a man who had taken the measure of this temptation better than anyone else because he himself had been a Pharisee, and exclusiveness had been his life. For this reason, when Christ called him by name on the road to Damascus, he was to dedicate his life to breaking with this temptation. Even in opposition to certain leaders of the Church, he was to make the universal interpretation of the Lord's message, the only true interpretation, prevail. It was because he had been Saul, that is, because he had realized to the full what were the needs of his time, that he was to become Paul, the missionary guide and the bearer of the Gospel to the pagans.

We now pass over several centuries, those wonderful yet terrible centuries in which cohorts of martyrs lived out the fundamental demand of the age—the demand for nonviolence and for conquering gentleness—in their tortured flesh by accepting, as one of their number put it, to be "ground between the teeth of the wild animals into the

white bread of Christ". Through them, the Revolution of
the Cross had succeeded. But the world in which the Gospel
had taken root was plunging into the abyss. Ruined
internally by its own betrayals, even more than by the
attacks of the barbarians, a whole society was collapsing.
Who were fully alive to the drama? The saints like Jerome,
Paulinus of Nola, John Chrysostom and Ambrose. These
at least had no illusions. But, at the same time, they refused
to give way to the temptation, then haunting so many
minds, to stampede in panic. Look at the old bishop who
is dying in Hippo, in a city besieged by the barbarian
hordes and stalked by plague: what is he doing? As he hews
out, over the space of ten years, a monumental work in
which the world, eager to be born, is made to spring from
the world now dying, St Augustine is writing his *City of
God*, the book of the Christendom which is to come.

And now this Christendom was born. Saints like
Columba, Boniface, Remigius, Avitus, Gregory the Great
and the converting queens Clotilde and Radegunde had
risked their lives to overcome the chaos left by the barbarians. Christendom had come into being, because, in
Ozanam's memorable phrase, the Church "passing over
to the barbarians" had succeeded in baptizing them. But
this was not enough: it was neccssary to give a Christian
meaning to power, and to order a baptized, but still far
from Christian world, according to the principles of the
Gospel. It was at this moment that St Bernard appeared,
to become the witness and guide for his age, in a way that
perhaps no one else had ever been—arbitrator of Europe,
counsellor of kings and popes, and Dante's chosen guide
in his journey to the regions of Hell, which are the
regions of sinful man—this was Bernard of Clairvaux,
knight and saint.

But then a new element in history comes into play. The

evolution of manners and of the economic system speedily brought about the ruin of feudalism, and, at the same time, endangered the virtues of the knight. The great subversion was being prepared—the subversion which Péguy was to express perfectly as, "Money become the master instead of God". Once again it was a saint, and a saint of exceptional greatness, who arose, after seeing within himself, in the depths of his own accomplice heart, the terrible dangers besetting the soul through money. He was the judge of the sin of his age, but he also became the guide for his contemporaries by suggesting to them, or, better, by embodying before them, the ideal of absolute poverty, of the total renunciation of wealth. You will have recognized him by now, St Francis, the Poverello of Assisi.

It would be easy to go on like this. What St Paul, St Augustine, St Bernard, St Francis of Assisi and so many other had done in their age, was equally what St Ignatius did when he reacted against the moral failings in the Church, which had determined the Protestant revolution, and formed his army of Christ, specially built to fight on every field where the "battle of the two standards" was being fought.

This was also what St Vincent de Paul did, in the violent and unjust French society which he knew exceptionally well, when he became a witness to the charity of Christ. This was also what saints like Alphonsus de Liguori and Paul of the Cross, who preached nothing but Jesus crucified, did in an Italy dedicated to extraordinary frivolities. And we can see the same thing quite near to us in the much maligned nineteenth century, when the rôle of sanctity was perhaps more important and more decisive than ever before, in the radiant simplicity of the Curé d'Ars in face of intellectual pride, in the limitless charity of Don Bosco, Père Chevrier and St Joseph Cottolengo in face of the

growing harshness of an inhuman world, and in the supernatural silence and mystical uselessness of a small nun
hidden in the Carmel of Lisieux, in face of man's own
betrayal of himself in an age fascinated by speed and
efficiency.

I hope that this rather odd atmosphere of an honours
list which this survey of Christian history has assumed will
be forgiven. But the inescapable truth is that holiness has
a place in this history such that to refuse to recognize it
would be to condemn oneself not to understand this history
at all. Holiness is the chief means of action among us used
by God.

Why is it that such an obvious truth is not always
recognized? The reason is that the witness of sanctity has
something disconcerting, and even, very often, something
scandalous, about it. And we do not even have to think
of some of the saints who pushed their challenge to the
world to extremes, like St Paul of the Cross, for example,
who scourged himself in public until he ran with blood,
and who had himself hung on a cross, so that he could
bring the realization of what Christ accepted to undergo
for the salvation of all quite literally within arm's reach
of his audience; or, to take a less horrifying example, like
St Francis who took off his clothes in front of the bishop
of Assisi, and who, on another occasion, compelled one
of his religious to eat the droppings of an ass for having
kept some tiny morsel of food for himself; or like St
Benedict Labre who, by not washing and by allowing lice
to flourish undisturbed on his hairy skin, brought home
quite clearly to his contemporaries of the eighteenth century
that, in spite of all their satins and flounces, they would be
eaten up by worms.

But even when it is not pushed as far as this, the paradox
of holiness is no less striking. Every man who really speaks

to us in God's name startles us and shocks us: this was already true of the prophets of Israel—they, too, we must remember, did odd things, like walking naked down the street. The truth is that a saint is a scandal; the existence of holiness is a scandal, in the normally accepted sense of the word; it produces, as the dictionary says, "a troublesome commotion". To some, it seems an absurdity; in others, it inspires a sort of contemptuous pity, or perhaps drives them to attempt to explain it and justify it on purely human grounds.

Voltaire's comment on St Vincent de Paul is famous: "Monsieur Vincent is the saint for me, because he is the saint of human misery." We must be fair, however, and thank the patriarch of Ferney for his comment, for it is presumably because of what he said that the founder of the Vincentians and of the Daughters of Charity appears with St Louis and Joan of Arc in the very short list of saints in our very secular primary manuals. We can, however, be certain that Monsieur Vincent himself would not have been entirely happy with the formula. To think that he was a saint because he had, as we now say, the social sense, because he organized soup for the people and orphanages for abandoned children, because he set up a sort of anticipation of modern charity organizations like Caritas, is to reduce him to the admittedly useful and worthy rôle of a director general of Social Security, but it is not to understand his vocation in any way. Henri Bremond made this profound remark about him: "He did not become a saint because he was charitable, but he was charitable because he was a saint." The effectiveness of the saints, even when it is startling by worldly standards, does not spring from social, political, or even merely moral intentions. If we judge it from these points of view, we shall quite simply fail to understand it. We should simply be falling in with the ideas of enlightened despots like

Frederick II and Joseph II (who were, precisely, Voltaire's friends) for whom there were two categories of religious: the first sort, who were tolerated, were teachers and nurses, and had a certain usefulness; the second, who were occupied solely in prayer, had to be eliminated because they were useless!

The truth is that holiness is not justified by its results; it does not need somehow to be legitimized by them. It must even be conceded that holiness is an absurdity. It is clearly absurd to live on mouldy potatoes and to spend eighteen hours a day in the dark box of the confessional, as the Curé d'Ars did. It is absurd to sacrifice one's life, as so many missionary martyrs have done, to go and teach a few dozen Red Indians, or Maoris or Eskimos to stumble over the Lord's Prayer and the "Hail Mary". It is absurd, from a worldly point of view, to shut oneself up in a convent at the age of eighteen, never again to emerge except at death, or to go and live, all alone, among the Tuaregs of the Hoggar, as Charles de Foucauld did, without even the hope of baptizing any of them. The scandalous absurdity of holiness is a fact which Christians should not only deny, but which we should assert as an obvious fact. If the saints had not been absurd and scandalous, if they could be judged by the same standards as other beings, these men and women who, as we have seen, were supernaturally effective, would not have been what they were. They might have been alive to the needs of their age—people like that are never lacking—but they would not have given their own special reply to the enigmas posed by the Sphinx of history—that staggering, astounding reply which we hear from their lips. And it is that reply, in the end, which saves the world.

This is the eternal lesson of holiness—a lesson which can only be understood in the context in which I have attempted to place all these remarks by invoking Claudel's great image of the Jesuit dying so that Rodrigo and Prouhèze might once more find grace, and not be swallowed up in the abyss—the context of vicarious merit, and the communion of saints. It is because this exists, because it is true that, in a mysterious way, each one of us really shares in the great striving and the endlessly repeated sacrifices of all the saints of the Church, that we do not feel that we have been left alone in the darkness surrounding us which fills our hearts. To the follies and the disorders of man, the saints reply with the folly of the cross.

We are now faced by the question whether there still exist men and women in our society, in our threatened world where so many imperious or insidious voices keep on saying that God is dead, who oppose the folly of the cross to the folly of mankind and the order of Christ's charity to the disorders which are killing us.

Among those who have thought most deeply about the tragedy of our world there are many who have proclaimed that this is the real problem, and who, from the depths of their beings, have uttered an appeal for holiness, like a cry answering to an anguish that they can no longer bear. We remember the somewhat bantering passage in which Péguy said: "Saints of all kinds have been needed in the past, and today we need yet another kind." And Bergson knew, better than anyone else, that the famous "supplement of the soul" for which he called for men who were a prey to the technological revolution, could only be brought to us by the saints and mystics.

It was for sanctity that Saint-Exupéry—that lucid and almost despairing witness to a world that has betrayed love, and the author of *Le Petit Prince* and *La Citadelle*—cried out. "It is for the saints to speak", Gabriel Marcel wrote in his preface to a book which deals with one of the most

striking aspects of the horror of our age. And Simone
Weil, in her *Waiting on God*, marked a decisive stage in
her spiritual journey when she exclaimed: "The world today
needs saints, new saints, saints of genius."

Saints of genius. . . . Perhaps. If to have genius means
to dominate one's age, to understand it to the core, and to
create values rich with possibilities for the future, then
every saint has his own brand of genius. But we do not
ask the saints of our age to show genius for mathematics
or physics, and to be capable of splitting the atom or of
sending a rocket to the moon—we already have more
than enough of those! Nor do we ask them to show a
genius for political and social sciences, and to be capable
of bringing order to our world: that is not their task.
But we do dream of saints who will have the genius to
plumb the depths of our misery and to bring us consolation,
to feel, and to make us feel, the anguish of those thousands
of beings who are slowly dying of hunger on our laden
earth, to share and to make us share, in the battle for
truth and justice which millions of souls are waging in
silence, to know, and to make us know, that if the "wind
of abandon," of which Gertrude von Le Fort has spoken,
is sweeping our age, we ourselves have not been abandoned.

If an inquiry were carried out in this field like those in
which the Gallup Institutes specialize, we might see that
this desire for holiness is much more widespread than we
think. There are so many signs of it that we shall only be
able to pick out one or two at random.

What are the countless readers of Edith Stein, Thomas
Merton and Simone Weil looking for in their works? Can
it simply be strange documents about curious lives full of
odd incident? Why is the America where technical skills
are triumphant also the America where Trappist abbeys
are increasing at a speed which the twelfth century would

have appreciated? Why are such crowds thronging the
huge esplanades of Lourdes and Fatima? Why are there
hermits, like Fr Peyriguère, setting off to become recluses
in the middle of the desert or in inaccessible mountains?
Why are films about saints, as producers realize full well,
so popular? Why are so many people making the journey
to Padre Pio in his monastery? Even when it takes on
odd, not to say scarcely admissible forms, this appetite
for holiness is an inescapable fact of daily observation.
And we have no right to reject this evidence.

Do you remember the words which Suger wrote to
St Bernard shortly before he died—Suger, the abbot of
Saint-Denis and the first minister of the two kings of
France, Louis VI and Louis VII? "If only I could see your
face just once before I return to God," he said, "I should
leave this miserable world in greater security." Is this
not our cry, too? Do we not also long to see the face of a
saint appear before us?

But perhaps our cry has already been answered. Perhaps,
even though we do not take sufficient notice of the fact,
holiness has already appeared among us in forms and
characteristics which, even so, have been clearly revealed
to us. Perhaps there are saints among us whom we are
unable to recognize but who will one day be seen to have
played that part in the dialectic of our time which has
always been the part played by holiness.

Nevertheless, without wishing to anticipate the decisions
of the Church, can we not already recognize the eternal
face of sanctity in a few concrete examples?

We think of Fr John Tong, the hero of Chinese Catholicism. It is now ten years since he was arrested and
arraigned before a Communist tribunal where he dared to
proclaim his complete faith in Christ, and his unrepentant
fidelity to the Church, and to protest in advance on behalf
of 3,700,000 Catholics against the violence which might

be done to their consciences and against all the apostasies which this might produce. Fr John Tong, who disappeared the day after his trial, was never seen again.

We think, too, of Fr Michael Favreau, a priest of the *Mission Ouvrière* of Bordeaux, who, in the enthusiasm of his twenty-five years, wished to share all the pains and all the anguish of the poorest working class. He became a docker among dockers, just as Paul had made himself a Greek among Greeks; one very tiring day, however, he voluntarily took the place of a companion, even more tired than himself and the father of a family, in a dangerous piece of work; a few moments later, when a load of wood toppled over on him, there remained only a broken body and his blood splashed about.

Lastly, and above all, we think of Fr Maximilian Kolbe, who will perhaps soon be beatified, whose exemplary figure embodied the most decisive of protests against the horror of our world in which, as his father St Francis said, "love is no longer loved". We think of that scene, worthy of the Acts of the Martyrs, in Auschwitz concentration camp, when hostages listed for death were being called out; he stepped from the ranks and asked, almost demanded, to die instead of another poor man who was in tears as he called out for his wife and children. We think of his solitary death in the hunger bunker.

In face of examples like these, anything we can say is empty—it is all mere literature. We are left to ponder in silence and prayer this mystery of Christ present in our time, as he has been in every other, of Christ present in his saints.

HENRI DANIEL-ROPS
of the *Académie Française.*

CHAPTER I

PAUL OF TARSUS, APOSTLE OF THE WORLD

Jesus of Nazareth had been dead for nineteen years; he had died, risen again and ascended into heaven, where he was now seated in glory at the right hand of the Father. In Jerusalem, the brethren were assembled. Among them, with the apostles and the elders, were Simon, who had been known as Peter ever since Jesus had given him the name, and the younger of the two Jameses—James the Less— who was a cousin to the Nazarene. Peter was the head of the whole Church, the rock on which the Master had willed it to be founded; James was the head of the community of Jews who had recognized the crucified preacher as the Messias, the Son of the living God.

The brethren were waiting for envoys from Antioch and Syria, with Paul and Barnabas at their head, who were due to arrive soon. A serious matter had been the cause of their journey. If the discussion about to take place were to turn out badly, the unity of the Church would be compromised; discord would scatter those who had been united by the Saviour. Christ's message might even be altered to such an extent that his faithful followers would henceforth be nothing more than a tiny, obscure sect in Israel. The hour was a grave one, in this the forty-ninth year of the new era inaugurated by Christ, in which the

Council of Jerusalem—the first full assembly of Christians —was about to open.

All through this anxious wait, the apostles and the oldest disciples—the men who had known the Lord, and who had listened and spoken to him—went over in their minds the memory of those years, those terrible years, but years which their hearts held dear, which they had spent among the people for whom Jesus, their Messias, had been sacrificed as a victim, and who had harshly persecuted them, his faithful followers.

Peter and James were thinking of that moment on the Mount of Olives, when the voice of the Beloved had rung for the last time in their ears: "The Holy Spirit will come upon you", he had told them, "and you will receive strength from him; you are to be my witnesses in Jerusalem and throughout Judaea, in Samaria, yes, and to the ends of the earth."

They remembered. But had they completely understood? "To the ends of the earth. . . ." This meant, in Aramaic, that their witness had to be taken to all men, and not only to the Jews; and there was no need—this was what had caused the difficulty—for Gentiles converted to the new faith to be compelled, in consequence, to practise the observances of the Old Law; Jesus had not commanded this, as he certainly would have done if he had seen any necessity for it. It was precisely because some brethren had come from Judaea to the Christian communities of Antioch, and had publicly decreed that it was necessary, in order to be saved, to accept the Mosaic practice of circumcision, that Paul and Barnabas were now coming to deny the assertion in front of Peter and James, who seemed not at all decided to give way on this point.

Simon Peter and James, the son of Alphaeus, however, could not have forgotten the day when they were gathered together in the upper room with John, the other James and Andrew, Philip and Thomas, Bartholomew and Matthew, Simon the Zealot and Jude, Matthias (whom they had just elected to take the place of Judas Iscariot) and Mary the mother of Jesus. A sound had suddenly come from heaven, like that of a strong wind blowing, and the whole house had been shaken; tongues of fire had come to rest on each of them, and they had begun to speak in all sorts of languages; when the Jews of the Dispersion heard them, Jews who were gathered in Jerusalem for the feast of Pentecost, Parthians, Medes, Elamites, Jews who lived in Mesopotamia and Cappadocia, in Pontus and Asia, in Phrygia and Pamphylia, in Egypt and in the parts of Libya round Cyrene, visitors from Rome, Cretans and Arabians, they said: "Are not they all Galileans speaking? How is it that each of us hears them talking his own native tongue? ... They have had their fill of new wine."

Peter had spoken to them, and had ended his speech with this exclamation: "Let it be known, then, beyond doubt, to all the house of Israel, that God has made him Master and Christ, this Jesus whom you crucified."

Peter was a Jew, and intended to speak only to Jews; and yet, a little later, under the inspiration of the Holy Spirit, he stated: "You will receive the gift of the Holy Spirit. This promise is for you and for your children, and for all those, however far away, whom the Lord our God calls to himself. ... Save yourselves from this false-minded generation."

Indeed, the man whom Jesus had appointed to be the head of his Church firmly believed at this moment that the reception of Christ's baptism did not dispense anyone from observing the Law promulgated by Moses, and that, to become a Christian, it was also necessary in some way to be a Jew. But Paul thought differently.

Entirely on his own, Paul had understood from the very beginning. But a direct intervention on God's part was needed for Peter's eyes to open—for Peter was no genius. The divine power, acting on Peter's mind, had revealed itself at Caesarea, and Peter had not forgotten. He had travelled from Lydda to Joppa, where Dorcas, a woman rich in good works, had died. Peter was taken to her deathbed, where he knelt down and prayed; then he said: "Dorcas, rise up", and Dorcas got up, and many learnt to believe.

Cornelius, a centurion in the Italian cohort which was then stationed in Caesarea, already believed. At this time, an angel appeared to him and ordered him to send some-one to the house of Simon the tanner, in Joppa, to fetch another Simon, who was surnamed Peter. Cornelius obeyed the angel.

At about the sixth hour, when the messengers were nearing the tanner's house, down by the seashore, Simon Peter, who was praying on the house-top, had a vision: he saw heaven opening and an unfolded sheet let down, full of all the beasts of the earth, animals, reptiles and birds; a voice told him to kill and eat. Peter protested, saying that he could not eat anything which was unclean, but three times the voice replied to him: "It is not for you, Peter, to call anything unclean which God has made clean."

The vision disappeared and, immediately afterwards, the Spirit informed the leader of the apostles that the messen-gers from Cornelius had arrived, and ordered him to follow them. So Peter left with them for Caesarea, accepted the centurion's hospitality, and told the Gentiles who were gathered in the house: "It is forbidden for a Jew to consort with one of another race, but God has been showing me that we ought not to speak of any man as unclean. This is why I am here. What do you want of me?"

Cornelius replied: "We are assembled in the presence of God ready to listen to whatever charge the Lord has given you." Then Peter said: "I see clearly enough that God makes no distinctions between man and man; he welcomes anybody, whatever his race, who fears him and does what piety demands. . . . Everyone who has faith in God is to find remission of sins through his name."

While he was speaking to them in this way, the Holy Spirit fell on all those who were listening to his message, and they began to speak in every tongue. Peter declared that baptism could not be refused to those who had received the Holy Spirit, and gave orders that they should all be baptized in the name of Jesus Christ.

When he returned to Jerusalem, he was attacked by the brethren, who violently reproached him for having consented to associate with pagans. But Peter exclaimed: "If God had made them the same free gift, which he made to us when faith in the Lord Jesus had gone before it, who was I, what power had I, to stay God's hands?"

The baptism of the centurion Cornelius and of his companions, which the Holy Spirit had suggested to the apostle Peter, marked the first, difficult stage on the apostolic road, along which Paul of Tarsus had thrown himself in order to go out to the Gentiles, and which was now leading him towards a critical encounter with the Judeo-Christian community at Jerusalem, which was still strictly bound to the Law of Moses, and completely imbued with the ancient prejudices of Israel. What sort of man was he, then, this Jew who was not built to the same pattern as the others, and who, on his own initiative, thought and acted differently from them? Only a short time before, it could have been said that he was the most Jewish of all men, even though he had seen the light of day outside the territory of Palestine, and that he was the bitterest enemy that the Christians had.

The date of his birth is not known for certain; he was probably born four or five years after Jesus had died and risen again; thus, on the eve of the assembly at

Jerusalem, he was less than forty years old. He had been born at the gates of Cilicia, at the extreme north-east point of the Mediterranean, in Tarsus, a port protected by the length of the Taurus, and bathed by the Cydnus at that point along the Asiatic coast where its waters flow into the sea.

The town, which was very old, was cosmopolitan; Greeks were the most numerous race there, but Jews were also fairly numerous. Paul's parents—he was still called Sha-ul, or Saul, then—came from Galilee; they belonged to the tribe of Benjamin; rich merchants, like most of the Jews who had settled in foreign lands, they enjoyed the *jus civitatis*, the right of Roman citizenship, which was a considerable privilege; Paul was always to behave as a loyal citizen of Rome.

An Israelite by race and faith, and a Roman by political adoption, he became a Greek by culture: Tarsus was a hellenistic university town. In spite of this, however, Paul's mind was not marked by any pagan influence; from adolescence, he had borne—and he was always to keep— the indelible imprint of militant Judaism: his father was a Pharisee, belonging to the very strictest sect. When he was fifteen, Paul went to Jerusalem to study the Torah; there he had Gamaliel for his master, and received his initiation into the finest subtleties of dialectic under the scholarly rabbi. Deeply imbued with the traditions of the chosen people, but having lived in daily contact with Gentiles, Paul of Tarsus grew up at the meeting-place of two worlds, both familiar to him. And this was to explain everything.

At first, he denied that Christ was God and Messias, looking upon him merely as an impostor, and he persecuted those who followed him; he had publicly approved of the martyrdom of the deacon Stephen and, tracking down the Christians right into their own homes, he had them imprisoned. He was on his way to Damascus entrusted by

the High Priest with dragging the brethren of that city
back to Jerusalem in chains. The rest of the story is best
told in the words of the Acts of the Apostles:

> Then, on his journey, when he was nearly at Damascus,
> a light from heaven shone suddenly about him. He fell to
> the ground, and heard a voice saying to him, Saul, Saul,
> why dost thou persecute me? Who art thou, Lord? he asked.
> And he said, I am Jesus, whom Saul persecutes. ... And he,
> dazed and trembling, asked, Lord, what wilt thou have me
> do? Then the Lord said to him, Rise up, and go into the
> city, and there thou shalt be told what thy work is. ... When
> he rose from the ground he could see nothing, although his
> eyes were open, and they had to lead him by the hand, to
> take him into Damascus (Acts 9. 3–9).

His mission had been changed. Now as Paul of Tarsus
he belonged to Christ. In Damascus, Ananias laid his hands
on him: "Brother Saul, I have been sent by that Jesus who
appeared to you on your way as you came here; you are
to recover your sight and be filled with the Holy Spirit."

Paul was filled with the Holy Spirit and could see. He
preached Christ to the Jews of Damascus, escaped their
murderous madness and, on the testimony of Barnabas,
was acknowledged by the brethren in Jerusalem; he had a
discussion with the Hellenists, moderated their demands
(which were as excessive as those of the Judaizers) in his
concern for balance, and had to flee their anger; he took
ship at Caesarea, and returned to his home town of Tarsus;
Jesus, appearing to him a second time, had ordered him to
leave Jerusalem and had told him that he was going to
send him far away to the Gentiles. And indeed, Barnabas
soon took Paul with him to Antioch in Syria, on the river
Orontes. There they spent a year, preaching the Gospel to
the Greeks, and baptizing a great number of them. Then,
from Seleucia, they took ship for Cyprus, crossed to Pamphylia by sea from Paphos, and went up to Pisidian Antioch

where Paul declared to the Jews of the Dispersion, who were jealous at seeing the whole city hanging on his lips: "We were bound to preach God's word to you first; but now, since you reject it, since you declare yourselves unfit for eternal life, be it so; we will turn our thoughts to the Gentiles."

This was the sort of man he was, a blazing fire, which was to set the world alight. The whole world. All the earth. All the men whom Christ had come to redeem and whom Paul, opening the way for the Twelve and for their successors, would be the first to give to Christ.

And now he was going on his way to Jerusalem, in order to persuade, not Peter and James in particular, for they, like him, had been visited by the Spirit, but the assembled brethren, who were struck with blindness, that this conquest should not be aimed at making the Gentiles who had accepted the Gospel observe the Law of Moses in addition. Such an action on the part of this lofty Jew was an indication of the pure genius and the lustre of his soul, as well as of his courage: to accomplish his historic task, he was journeying towards insults, blows, and perhaps even death itself; in this, he was already a saint, for his fighting virtue verged on heroism. And through his virtue the Church was about to act.

But did he look like a hero? Not in the least. He was short, with a squat body, thickset shoulders, bandy legs, a skull bare of hair, bushy eyebrows which met in the middle, and a nose that betrayed his origin. But admittedly this graceless body hid a soul bursting with power and dazzling with light.

So Paul, breaking off his victorious journeys, was making his way towards Jerusalem, together with Barnabas. The task awaiting him was a difficult one, as he himself knew perfectly well; but it was also one of those tasks which he loved to tackle simply because of their difficulty; he had never been, and never would be, a man of easy struggles crowned by derisive successes, by victories without a future.

As Paul of Tarsus drew near to the city, he felt a little more certain of Peter and James. The fact that John was there, as he had learnt while he was travelling, finally re-assured him: Jesus' closest friend, who had known the Master's mind intimately, could only be on his, Paul's, side.

After leaving Antioch in Syria, the day after their quarrel with the Judaizers, Paul and Barnabas, accompanied by half a dozen of the brethren from Syria, travelled across Phoenicia, from Beirut to Mount Carmel, on horseback; now they were journeying towards Jerusalem, skirting the Roman province of Judaea near the coast.

They had left Sebaste on their left and seen the summit of Mount Garizim rise up in the east, and had left Samaria at Antipatris. Their gaze had lingered for a moment on Arimathea, the town in which Joseph, who had offered his new tomb to the Lord, had lived; after touching Lydda, they were journeying towards Emmaus, where fresh memories awaited them.

The Church was assembled in Jerusalem around Peter, James and John. Attended by the elders, the apostles welcomed Paul and Barnabas who, under a flood of questions, told the assembled brethren of the conquests which God had made with them among the Gentiles.

At this point, some newly baptized Christians who had come from the sect of the Pharisees intervened. "We must circumcise the Gentiles," they declared, "and order them to observe the Law of Moses."

The debate was opened. The apostles and the elders continued it behind closed doors. After a fairly lively exchange of opinions, Peter spoke:

> Brethren, you know well enough how from early days it has been God's choice that the Gentiles should hear the message of the gospel from my lips, and so learn to

believe. God, who can read men's hearts, has assured them of his favour by giving the Holy Spirit to them as to us. He would not make any difference between us and them; he had removed all the uncleanness from their hearts when he gave them faith. How is it, then, that you would now call God in question, by putting a yoke on the neck of the disciples, such as we and our fathers have been too weak to bear? It is by the grace of our Lord Jesus Christ that we hope to be saved, and they no less (Acts 15. 7–12).

Paul was filled with joy when he heard the head of the apostles speak in this way. How right he had been not to have expected anything else. Since Peter agreed with him, he contented himself, when the rest of the assembly did not dare to put forward any objections to these words, which defined the teaching of the Church on a point of crucial importance, with continuing, aided by Barnabas, the account of the miracles which God had willed to accomplish through them among the Gentiles. It was then James' turn to intervene. He said:

Listen, brethren, to what I have to say. Simon has told us, how for the first time God has looked with favour on the Gentiles, and chosen from among them a people dedicated to his name. This is in agreement with the words of the prophets, where it is written: Afterwards, I will come back, and build up again David's tabernacle that has fallen; I will build up its ruins, and raise it afresh; so that all the rest of mankind may find the Lord, all those Gentiles among whom my name is named, says the Lord, who is the doer of all this. God has known from all eternity what he does today. And so I give my voice for sparing the consciences of those Gentiles who have found their way to God; only writing to bid them abstain from what is contaminated by idolatry, from fornication, and from meat which has been strangled or has the blood in it. As for Moses, ever since the earliest times he has been read, sabbath after sabbath, in the synagogues, and has preachers in every city to expound him (Acts 15. 13–21).

Paul had no objection to this either: quite the contrary. James, like Peter, agreed with him on essentials; and it was the Spirit—Paul was convinced of this—who had inspired both of them to speak. There could not be any real disagreement among the three of them, since, as everyone well knew, Jesus was present among them.

It was surely Jesus who again inspired them to name some brethren from Jerusalem to accompany Paul and Barnabas to Antioch; Judas, who was called Barsabas, and Silas were chosen; they would be the bearers of the message which Peter and James were to draw up, with Paul's approval:

> To the Gentile brethren in Antioch, Syria and Cilicia, their brethren the apostles and presbyters send greetings.
>
> We hear that some of our number who visited you have disquieted you by what they said, unsettling your consciences although we had given them no such commission; and therefore meeting together with common purpose of heart, we have resolved to send you chosen messengers, in company with our well-beloved Barnabas and Paul, men who have staked their lives for the name of our Lord Jesus Christ. We have given this commission to Judas and Silas, who will confirm the message by word of mouth. It is the Holy Spirit's pleasure and ours that no burden should be laid upon you beyond these, which cannot be avoided; you are to abstain from what is sacrificed to idols, from blood-meat and meat which has been strangled, and from fornication. If you keep away from such things, you will have done your part. Farewell (Acts 15. 23–9).

Paul and Barnabas, together with Judas and Silas, once more took the road for Antioch.

We read in the Acts of the Apostles that they "called the multitude together and delivered the letter to them; and they, upon reading it, were rejoiced at this encouragement. Judas and Silas, for they were prophets too, said much to encourage the brethren and establish their faith;

they stayed there for some time before the brethren let them go home, in peace, to those who had sent them. Paul and Barnabas waited at Antioch, teaching and preaching God's word" (Acts 15. 30–5).

Paul of Tarsus preached that holy word to the Gentiles, to Galatians, Ephesians, Colossians, Thessalonians, Philippians, Corinthians, Athenians and Romans, until the day of his death when he suffered martyrdom on the Ostian Way. By his journey to Jerusalem he had made a decisive contribution to the opening of a path along which the Church was to follow; it was to lead her on to the universal conquest of souls, although this would never invalidate the promise made by Yahweh to the people of Israel. Thus, thanks to his wonderful balance, he brought about the harmony which Christ had wanted to establish between the Old Law and his own message; and this unity was founded under the sign, and in the sole name, of love. Thus, at the dawn of Christianity, the Church acted through St Paul.

CHAPTER II

STRUGGLE AND DEATH OF AUGUSTINE THE BISHOP

Hippo lay under the siege. Augustine was on the point of death. A year before this Numidian spring—the 430th of the Christian era—flowered in the burning African sun, Genseric's tawny-haired Germans had crossed the Pillars of Hercules and hurled themselves on their prey: Rome's granary, orchard and vineyard, trampled underfoot, had begun to burn.

They came from the lands frozen by the ice of the Vistula, and had crossed Gaul and Spain in a lightning raid; they were Barbarians, pagan savages: all that Arius' debased Christianity had added to their ancestral beliefs was a few more perversions and a few more curious rites.

The court of Ravenna had sent Count Boniface, a political general, to meet them. His legions, Goth mercenaries, had been swept from the field. Boniface had fled, and had come to take refuge in Hippo. There the Vandals beleaguered him. Augustine's city was marked out for death.

Augustine himself, the bishop of the city, was shivering, not with fear, but with a malignant fever. His own days also were numbered. But the flame which had consumed him ever since the passionate days of his adolescence was slow to flicker out. He was the soul of the defence, the soul of Hippo. Christ's spirit was stamped on his features, vibrated in his voice, trembled beneath his pen and beat in the impulses of his heart. In a land running with blood, ravaged by fire, crushed by fear and plunged into darkness, his mere presence conjured up peace, brought joy and kindled the light of heaven, the light which was burning within him, and which he gave to all.

Augustine was a son of Africa. He had been born in Tagaste, in the middle of the fourth century (Tagaste is now known as Souk Ahras, just as Hippo has become Bône, and Cirta, Constantine). At that time, they were towns in Numidia, a region to the west of the Roman province of Africa, where Carthage still kept its former glory.

The extreme climate and the blood of a violent race had shaped the intelligent boy to excess; he was violent but disinclined to effort; Monica, his Christian mother, with the obstinate sweetness of the saints, was to fill him, without his realizing it, with supernatural gifts. When he came to Carthage to study rhetoric, Augustine was more concerned to sacrifice to Venus than to Christ, whose baptism he, like his father, Patricius, had refused. But he bore within him the seed of God in the triple form of restlessness, a spirit of inquiry, and that burning thirst for love which he was later to evoke in that gloriously immodest admission, "I loved to love".

Esotericism naturally tempted him: with his Manichean friends, he took a delight in it. Then, in his ambition, he felt drawn to Rome, where he led an aimless life. Milan called him, and he took up residence there. God awaited him in that city, hidden beneath the distinguished features of Ambrose, the bishop of Milan.

Ambrose, a noble patrician, an influential politician, a

venerated prelate, a scholarly intellect and a sublime orator, who had the ear of the emperor, and who had gained the votes of the people, impressed Augustine. He felt shaken to the core of his being. The ambiguous atmosphere of moral wildness and intellectual feverishness, which had enveloped him until then, was purified and healed beneath the breath of this man of God. He threw himself headlong into Plato and Plotinus, and there he at last discovered the universe fashioned by the divine Word, in its transcendence and splendour. God was there. "I was drawn to you," he was to write later, "by your beauty." With his mother, who had rejoined him, and his intimate friends, he withdrew to the monastic retreat of Cassiciacum to prepare for baptism, which he received from Ambrose on April 25th, 387. When, a little later, at Ostia, after an ecstasy which had raised them both from the ground, Monica took leave of Augustine to finish her journey of love which led her straight to heaven, she left to the Church the saint whose genius was to make it triumph over the combined attacks of heresy and barbarism.

Four years had passed, years which Augustine had spent in silence at Tagaste, when he came one day to Hippo. The Christian people acclaimed him: "Augustine for the priesthood!" There and then, he was ordained by Valerius, the old bishop, and became his coadjutor; when the bishop died in 396, Augustine suceeded him in the see. Possidius, later bishop of Calama, has left a description of this event, written in his picturesque style: "Thus it was that this shining lamp, which sought nothing more than darkness and solitude, found itself set on the lampstand." From this high position it was to light the Christian world, which is still dazzled today, some sixteen hundred years later, by its light.

Thirty-four consuming years in the apostolate had prepared Augustine for his supreme task, which was to be to fight, among his people, against the unleashed hordes of Arius. Could he thus crown his life's work—which had been to fight with pen and voice and action against heresy— with even greater lustre? He had laid his former friends the Manicheans low, had crossed swords first with the followers of Donatus, whose defeat he was patiently pre- paring, and then with the followers of Pelagius, who proved to be equally incapable of standing up to his blows. In this way, he had not only fully preserved the purity of the Christian faith, but he had also provided it with weapons which would serve to preserve it from any future attack— an inexhaustible theological and philosophical arsenal, the breastplate, shield, lance and sword of the Church of Christ, which she can always use in our times to face her new enemies and defeat them.

The year 410 marks the beginning of Augustine's final battle, which was to face him with his most formidable enemy. This time error assumed the form of the numberless hosts of Goths, who were galloping over the Empire: Rome had just fallen, and a whole world, soon to be buried beneath its ruins, was on the brink of death; the hour of the barbarians had tolled out on the dial of history, and the echoes had reached as far as the blue skies of Hippo, striking its bishop to the heart.

What did he do? Once again, battle was being offered him, even imposed on him. He accepted it, furbished his weapons and prepared to fight. Was history being written before him in letters of blood? In docile obedience to his genius he was to found a philosophy of history, and to begin his great masterpiece: in letters of fire, on the still blank pages of the book of man, Augustine began to write *The City of God*. The first book opened with the sack of Rome by Alaric's bands; at the end of thirteen years of work, as the climax to the drama of the human race, the twenty-second book contains the grandiose annals of the last Judgement.

And now Genseric's Vandals were nearing Hippo; cities blazed; men fled. The bishops themselves precipitated the flight, turning the fear, which was taking hold of their flocks, into panic, and, what was a thousand times worse, abandoning the souls entrusted to their care. At this, Augustine turned aside from the page of the *City of God* which he had begun, and, on his parchment, wrote to his defaulting colleagues to remind them of their duties; to Honorius, for example, he wrote this letter, the most famous of them all, a letter which seemed to be addressed to all the prelates of Africa:

> Why are they so ready to believe on every occasion that they ought to obey the precept to fly from town to town, and are not afraid that they might be the hireling who takes to flight as soon as he sees the wolf coming because he has no concern for his flock? Why do they not try to reconcile those two commandments of the Lord, which are both equally valid, one allowing or commanding flight, and the other censuring it or condemning it? Yet it is not difficult to make these two passages of the Gospel agree. The ministers of Christ are permitted to flee from those regions where persecution is raging, either when there is nobody left there who needs their ministry, or when the faithful who stay behind can be cared for by other ministers who do not have the same reason for leaving their Church. It was in this way that the Apostle fled when, pursued by a government which was looking for him, he was let down in a basket from a window. There were other ministers at Damascus who were not compelled, like St Paul, to flee, and so the Church was not left abandoned. The same thing happened with St Athanasius, the bishop of Alexandria. When the emperor Constantius was seeking to seize him, he fled; however, there were other ministers left who did not abandon the Catholic people of Alexandria. When the people remain behind while the ministers flee, and thus deprive the faithful of the support of their ministry, do we not have the case of the culpable flight of hirelings who

have no concern for the sheep? Then the wolf will come, and the wolf will not merely be a man who will persecute the faithful, but will be the Devil, who will often drive those Christians, deprived of the daily sacrament of the Body of the Lord, into apostasy. In this way, your ignorance, rather than your knowledge, will be the cause of the death of your still weak brother, for whom Christ died.

As for those who, in circumstances like these, are not deceived by error, but overcome with fear, why do they not fight their fear by begging the Lord for mercy and help, so that they will avoid falling into incomparably more terrifying evils? This is what would happen if only their hearts were aflame with the fire of charity, instead of being clouded by the smoke of the passions of this world, for charity says: "Does anyone feel a scruple? I share it; is anyone's conscience hurt? I am ablaze with indignation." Let us pray, then, that he who urges charity on us should give it to us. And animated by that charity, let us be more afraid of Christ's sheep perishing spiritually beneath the sword of spiritual iniquity, than of their perishing bodily beneath the sword of the Barbarians, since, in one way or the other, they will have to die sooner or later. Let us fear that the purity of our faith might be lost through the corruption of our inner feelings, rather than fearing that violence might soil women in their flesh; for violence cannot harm chastity as long as the soul remains chaste, and the soul cannot lose any of its purity in face of the exercise of brutal force against the body, provided that the will is reduced to accepting it without consenting to it. Let us be more afraid of bringing about the ruin of those living stones of the temple of the Lord by our desertion, than of seeing the wood and stone of worldly buildings burning before our eyes. And, finally, let us be more afraid of seeing the members of the body of Jesus Christ dying for lack of spiritual food, than of seeing our bodies exposed to the tortures and cruelty of the Barbarians.

Day by day, the threat was becoming clearer; Hippo, Christ's African stronghold, was to undergo Genseric's attack. To strengthen his frightened flock, nearly every day Augustine made the vaults of his church ring with the echoes of his powerful voice.

Already, once before, when Rome had fallen, he had drawn the lesson of history from that bloody collapse in his 295th sermon, which brings back to us the sovereign tone and rhythm of his homilies, and the profound teaching they contain.

You can see, my dearly beloved, what sort of things God holds out to his servants in this present life, so that they can merit the glory which is one day to be revealed in us, a glory with which the sufferings of this life, no matter how great, cannot be compared. "I do not count these sufferings" said St Paul, "as the measure of that glory which is to be revealed in us."

If this is the case, let no one give way to carnal thoughts, for this is not the time; the world is tottering ... and our flesh is in the press, so that the spirit might flow from it and shine out. There are some who say: "Peter's body lies in Rome; Paul's body lies in Rome; Lawrence's body is in Rome; the bodies of many other holy martyrs lie in Rome; and even so Rome is in misery, Rome has been laid waste; it has been beaten down, crushed and set on fire. Plague, famine and the sword bring carnage and death to the city: where are the tombs and memories of the martyrs now? What do you say about that?" I am saying that Rome has to suffer the worst of evils; of what use are the memories of the apostles? The memories of the apostles may be alive in the city of Rome, but they are not alive in your heart. Would to God that they were alive in your heart, for then you would not be speaking like this, and we should not have to listen to this foolish and carnal talk from a man who has been called to the life of the spirit. For the moment, what I should like to teach you is not wisdom but patience. Be patient, the Lord wills it. And why does he will it, you ask? Wait a while, and then you will know his secret; for the moment, prepare yourself to obey courageously. God wants you to bear trials; put up with what he wants, and then he will give you what you want. And yet, my brothers, this is something that I dare to say, and you will listen to me gladly, if you hold to the first commands of obedience and if you bear with gentle and calm patience the effects of the divine will. We do not undergo what is pleasant, but we love it; but we put up with what is unpleasant, while we find joy in what is pleasurable. Think of the Lord your God, think of your leader, think of your model in life, your redeemer and your shepherd. "My Father (he said) if it is possible, let this chalice pass me by." Why was it that our Saviour first allowed his human will to come into play, and then immediately bent all his efforts to obedience? "Only (he said) as thy will is, not as mine is." Now listen to what he said to Peter: "When thou hast grown old, another shall gird thee, and carry thee where thou goest, not of thy own will." In Peter, he shows us the human will in its natural trembling in the face of death. But, because St Peter died without wishing it, are we to say that he was crowned against his will? Perhaps you, too, do not wish to lose what you possess, and yet you will have to leave it behind here on earth; take care that you yourselves do not remain with those goods which you will have to leave behind. You would not like to see either your son or your wife die before you. But, after all, even if the city of Rome had not been taken, would not one of you have still been the first to die? You would not like your wife to die before you; and your wife, similarly, would not like her husband to die before her: can God satisfy both of you? Leave it to him to arrange things as he wills; he knows how to bring order into what he has created. Be content to obey his will, for his will is great.

But I can see that, in your heart, you are saying: it was when the world was Christian that Rome was destroyed. Why do we have disasters like these in a Christian era? Who is saying these things? A Christian? If you are a Christian, tell yourself that it happened when God willed. But, you will say, what answer am I to give a pagan who insults me? What is it that he says to you? How does he insult you? This is how: while we offered sacrifices to our gods (the pagans say) Rome remained standing and flourished; but now that the sacrifice of your God is dominant, being offered everywhere, and now that it has taken the place of the sacrifices to our gods, which are forbidden and proscribed, see what disasters have fallen on Rome! Reply quite shortly to this pagan, in order to get rid of him: you yourself think differently from him. You were not called to attach yourself to the earth, but to gain heaven; you were not called to any temporal enjoyment, to any ephemeral and passing happiness, but to eternal life in the company of the angels. However, do not hesitate to reply to this man with his passionate desire for a totally sensual happiness, who is murmuring against the living and true God, and who wishes to adore devils, gods of wood and stone. As Roman history testifies, this is the third time that the city has been the prey of the flames. Yes, their own historians and writers agree in saying that this fire is the third which has caught the city of Rome. This city, which has just been burnt while the Christians were everywhere offering their sacrifices (as the pagans point out), had already twice been reduced to cinders while sacrifices were being offered to pagan deities. On one occasion, it was burnt by the Gauls, and only the Capitoline hill escaped the flames. After this, it was burnt down a second time by Nero, whether in a fit of fury or drunkenness, I do not know. On the command of Nero—Nero, the emperor of the city of Rome, a slave to idols and the butcherer of the apostles—the city was given to the flames. Why was this? What do you imagine the reason was? This man, drunk with power, and as proud as he was effeminate, wanted to have the pleasure of seeing the city burn. I want to see, he said, how the city of Troy was consumed by fire. So Rome was burnt on three separate occasions. What is the reason, then, for all this murmuring against God on account of a city which has so often been the victim of the flames?

In this closely knit argument, we can certainly see once more the former rhetorician of Carthage and Milan; today, we should call him a debater with a well prepared case, and that was what Augustine must have been at the end of his career, just as in the days of his youth. But we must not forget that his immediate audience were men who had a twofold threat hanging over them, and whom he had to persuade of the primacy of spiritual values, reminding them of what their real destiny was: thus, by his eloquence, he drew out the lesson of history, which can only be interpreted correctly by those who must believe that history itself is subject to the working out within us of the divine plan. This is a lesson which is valid for all ages of mankind, and particularly for our own, which Augustine, as early as the dawn of the fifth century, provided with directives justified as much by reason as by faith.

However, the threat became more pressing for the beings whose care was entrusted to him, care of their lives as well as care of their souls. Then, in the sermons which followed, he raised the tone of the discussion for them.

In the 302nd sermon, he said:

> Note this fact well, what passionate lovers this present life has, this life which is slipping away, this short, sad life; ah yes, what lovers she has! Because of her, it happens more often than not that a man will strip himself; he will be naked and go begging. You ask him why, and he replies: So that I can live. Whom have you loved, then, and where has your love led you? What can you say, poor lover, of this evil mistress of yours? What is there for you to say to the life which you have loved with such folly? Look, speak to her, caress her, if you can. What are you going to say to her? "I am naked; this is where your beauty has brought me." And she cries out to you: "I am ugly; how can you love me?" She cries out to you: "I am harsh; how can you embrace me?" She cries out to you: "I am inconstant; how can you pursue me?" Yes, this is how your mistress replies to you: "I shall not stay with you. After a few moments, I shall go. I have certainly been able to strip you, but I cannot give you happiness."

In his 347th sermon, in which he took the fear of God as his theme, Augustine comments at length on Isaias and on his definition of wisdom. This sermon is one of Augustine's best.

Wisdom! And was this not, in fact, the right moment, when Hippo, after Rome, was being threatened with ruin and death, for him to offer it as the supreme recourse to the men entrusted to him, whom he had the duty of preserving, less from death than from apostasy, when the time should come for the Vandals to impose their own law.

It was to exercise us in marching towards wisdom that Isaias descended, as if by steps, from wisdom to fear, that is, from the place of eternal peace to our present valley of tears, so that, as we do penance in sorrow, groaning and weeping, we should not be content always to go on suffering, groaning and weeping, but should raise ourselves from this valley to the spiritual mountain on which the holy city of Jerusalem, our mother for ever, is built, and enjoy a happiness which cannot be disturbed. Thus, it is wisdom above all that Isaias urges on us, wisdom, the indefectible light of the mind; but he adds understanding, as if he wished to reply to anyone who asked, that wisdom comes from understanding; and understanding from counsel; and counsel from fortitude; and fortitude from knowledge; and knowledge from piety; and piety from fear. In this way, we go from fear to wisdom, for fear is the beginning of wisdom; we go from this valley of tears to the mountain of peace.

Then, when we have reached our goal, we stop, rest, and triumph in security and peace. And what is this goal, if not Christ our Lord, for Christ is *the end of the law for everyone who believes*? And what is the wisdom of God if not Christ? So it is in him that all become wise, and in him that all become children of God, who do become so, and this is unmixed and everlasting peace. Thus, just as in Isaias, wisdom is the seventh gift which comes to those who are climbing the heights from which the Lord himself has come down to us in order to teach us, so he who lifts us up to these heights said in the seventh beatitude: "Blessed are the peace-makers; they shall be counted the children of God." In possession of promises like these, let us follow these steps which lead to the Lord, and let us suffer the pains and hardships of this world, without allowing ourselves to be beaten down by its fury. If we triumph over it, we shall enjoy everlasting peace.

We can pause for a moment to think of the sort of people to whom exhortations like this were addressed, and in what circumstances of time and place. Hippo was being beseiged; if its walls were to fall, fury would be unleashed on the people whom they protected, and not one of them would be spared by the Vandals. This is why Augustine, who had himself drawn near to the doors of death, tried to turn their minds away from this world built on violence alone, and to direct their terrified souls towards the eternal peace of heaven. There stood the City of God—immovable, incorruptible, and beyond the reach of anxiety, terror and grief. In his cell, during his nights of insomnia, Augustine finished correcting the accumulated pages of his work which was promised to posterity.

He had written in the fifth book:

If God had not granted the earthly glory of a flourishing empire to those who were not to receive eternal life in his heavenly City, in the company of his holy angels, the good actions and the virtues by which they strove to acquire that glory, would have gone without reward. But it was of those who do good in order to win the esteem of men that the Lord said: "Believe me, they have their reward already." It is true that these men sacrificed their private fortunes for the good of the State and to increase the income of the public treasury; it is true that they resisted avarice, that they provided for the well-being of their country by their disinterested counsels, that they were not inclined to debauchery, and that they did not commit any of the crimes covered by their laws; but they only practised all these virtues as the best road to honour, supreme authority and glory. For this reason, nearly every country held them in honour: they imposed the laws of their empire on a host of peoples, and today history still carries their renown into nearly all the countries of the world. They have no cause to complain of the justice of the sovereign and true God. They have received their reward.

Augustine's people did not look for their reward here on earth. They knew, since they had heard the words fall from their bishop's lips, where it was that their destiny was to find its fulfilment, and what was the crown awaiting them as a prize for their struggles on earth. But they were still weak and, day and night, the shouts of Genseric's warriors came to assail the ramparts, and always made their blood run cold with fear. Their weakness needed to be fortified, and their timorous hearts reassured. It was for them that Augustine again wrote:

Radagaisus, king of the Goths, had drawn near to Rome with a formidable army of Barbarians, and was threatening to kill off all the inhabitants when, in a single day, he was defeated so rapidly that the Romans, without suffering a single death, or even a single casualty, cut to pieces more than a hundred thousand men of his army, while Radagaisus himself, taken prisoner with his sons, was put to death as he deserved. After all, if this impious chieftain had entered the city, with that host of soldiers all as impious as himself, who would have received mercy at his hands? What martyr's tomb would he have honoured? In what man would he have feared the person of God? Whose blood would he have refrained from spilling, and whose chastity would he have respected? Above all, how these barbarians would have raised their voices in favour of their gods; in what an insulting and derisive manner would they have congratulated themselves on having gained the victory, and on having proved so powerful, because their king appeased the gods and made them favourable to himself by daily sacrifices—a thing which the Christian religion does not allow the Romans to do. And, in fact, as he was drawing near to the spot where the God of majesty struck him down by his power, and as the renown of his name spread everywhere, it was said in Carthage that the pagans believed, and loudly proclaimed, that with the help and protection of friendly gods, to whom it was said that they offered sacrifices every day, their king could never be beaten by men who no longer offered sacrifices to the gods of Rome, and did not allow such sacrifices to be offered. And these wretches did not thank the infinite goodness of God, who, resolving to punish guilty man by this barbarian invasion, had deigned to moderate his anger by so great an act of mercy that he had allowed this sudden and marvellous defeat, fearing that the Barbarian's victory would be attributed to the devils whom they invoked, and that this would unsettle weak minds.

But the defeat of Hippo was a possibility too; and death would follow close on its heels. In the thirteenth book of the *City of God*, Augustine depicted the face of death, and showed how a Christian should look at it—in the face, and without growing pale:

In the hour when bodily death, that is, the separation of the soul from the body, is undergone by the dying, it is not good for anyone at all. This power, which is contrary to nature, and which tears apart two substances united and interwoven into one living thing, makes itself felt harshly while the death agony is prolonged, until all internal feeling, produced by the union of soul and flesh, is completely destroyed. Undoubtedly, it sometimes happens that one single blow to the body, or the fainting of the soul, brings this torture to an end, and that death comes so swiftly that it arrives before anguish. However, no matter how this power, which makes itself felt so grievously in the dying as it takes away their feeling, may come, it will increase the merit of the sufferer, provided that it is borne with piety and faith, although it will not, as a consequence, cease to merit the name of suffering. Thus, if it is certain that death is the punishment for birth inflicted on all the descendants of the first man, it is turned into the glory of the new birth when it is endured for the sake of religion and of righteousness; and then, even while it is a retribution for sin, it can also sometimes obtain complete liberation from sin.

And now at last, in the fourteenth book, the two cities built by Augustine rise up, one dominating the other, and filling it with a divine light. Bodies wounded to death remain captive in the city below; souls liberated from these perishable bodies wing their way to the city above, where love has opened the doors for them:

> Thus, two loves have built two Cities: the love of self carried to contempt for God, the earthly City; and the love of God carried to contempt for self, the heavenly City. One glories in itself, the other in the Lord. One goes begging to men for its glory, the other places its highest glory in God, who is a witness to its conscience. One, puffed up with pride, lifts up its haughty head; the other says to its God: "You are my glory, and you lift up my head." In one, the princes are ruled by the passion to lord it over their subjects, or conquered nations; in the other, the citizens serve each other in charity, the leaders by caring for the good of those who are subordinates, and the subjects by obeying. The first, in the person of its powerful men, admires itself in its strength; the second says to its God: "I shall love you, Lord, who are all my strength." The wise men of the earthly City, who live according to men, do not seek for anything but the good of the body or of the mind, or even of both together; even those who have had the opportunity of knowing God, have not glorified him as their God, or, without giving thanks to him, have gone astray in the vanity of their thoughts, and their insensate hearts have been filled with darkness. Taking the name of wise men upon themselves—that is, lifting themselves up in their own wisdom, ruled as they are by pride—"they turned fools, and exchanged the glory of the imperishable God for representations of perishable man, of bird and beast and reptile". For they led the people into this sort of worship, or followed

them into idolatry, "reverencing and worshipping the creature in preference to the Creator, who is blessed for ever". In the heavenly City, on the contrary, the only wisdom that man knows is the wisdom of piety, which alone can offer legitimate worship to God, while waiting for its reward in the society of the saints when men will be associated to the angels themselves, in order that God may be all in all.

We read, in the works of Possidius, a priest of Hippo and later bishop of Calama:

> One day, while we were at table with Augustine, he said to us in the course of conversation:
> "In the presence of these calamities, I ask God to deliver this city from the siege or, if this is not his intention, to give his servants the courage that they need in order to carry out his will or, at the very least, to take me from this world and to receive me into his bosom."
> After he had said this, we, our coadjutors and all the clerics who were in the city offered, at his request, the same prayer to God Almighty. In the third month of the siege fever forced him to bed. He was suffering from an illness which was destined to be his last. No doubt the Lord had heard the prayer of his servant, for he obtained for himself, and for his city as long as he was alive, what he had demanded with tears.
> Right up to his last illness, he had never failed to preach the word of God in his church, with boundless ardour and courage, and with a spirit and a power of judgement which were as healthy as they were to the point. In the words of Scripture, he slept with his fathers, as we watched. We were, in fact, gathered around him, and our prayers were joined to his. He did not make a will, for he was so poor that he had nothing to bequeath.

Except, of course, the lesson of his life, and his immortal work, and so it was in this way, in face of heresy and violence, that the Church was at work through St Augustine.

CHAPTER III

BERNARD OF CLAIRVAUX, THE ARBITRATOR OF KINGS

The monk with the shaven head, clothed in coarse, white wool, who made his entry, on December 24th, 1146, into the Diet of Spires, where the German, Conrad, was about to receive the imperial crown, was regarded by Western Christendom as the chief counsellor of the emperor, the intellectual master of the pope, the censor of bishops, the arbitrator of princes, and the man whom God had given to his century to be its leader. Bernard, abbot of the Cistercian house of Clairvaux in Champagne, despite his multiple activities was before all else a monk; his saintliness and personality, rather than his intellectual calibre, made him a powerful personage in the Europe of his times. It is important, therefore, to set Bernard of Clairvaux' dominant influence over the men and the events of his century in its proper context.

We remember that he had sprung from a noble soil, and from a noble race, at a time when nobility was the guarantee of greatness, and a factor in a man's effectiveness; this is only an historical view, but it is one which we should not neglect: if Bernard had sprung from the working class, and if he had not been born in Burgundy, he would never have been able, in the twelfth century, to carry out the mission which God had entrusted to him.

He was born, at this turning-point in medieval society, in Fontaines-lès-Dijon, during the summer of 1090, of Tescelin le Sor, or le Roux, who was a knight, and Aleth de Montbard, who belonged to the line of the dukes of Lorraine: Bernard could deal with any lord of his time on equal terms, and this is by no means a trivial factor when we consider his action in the world.

When he was twenty years old, his choice fell neither on politics nor on war; nor did he choose the pleasures of the world, to which his brilliant gifts, his breeding and his ability to please seemed to destine him; he made up his mind to choose the strictest monastery he could find, and went and presented himself, together with twenty-nine friends or relations of like mind, at the door of the new monastery which the Cluniac, Robert of Molesmes, had founded in the middle of an unwholesome swamp in the woods of Cîteaux. Bernard of Fontaines became a monk. Two years later the abbot of Cîteaux, St Stephen Harding, bade him choose a place for a further foundation and he established an abbey at Clairvaux whence his influence soon spread, it is fair to say, all over Europe. It was from the monastery of Clairvaux, founded in conditions of terrible severity, that Bernard was to take wing, pointing out the way that Western Christendom was to follow, and keeping it to it. In this way, during his supernatural career, Bernard was to bear to the men of his age what he himself possessed in superabundance, divine grace.

Bernard made his monastic profession in June 1113. When, some two years later, his abbot, Stephen Harding, appointed him to go, at the head of twelve monks from Cîteaux, to found a new monastery, he had been just three years in the religious life, and was twenty-three years old. It could almost be said that he was still a novice, still almost a child; and yet, on that day in June 1115 when he planted the foundation cross of the abbey of Clairvaux in the valley of Absinthe (the bitter site), he was already, by the grace of God, a complete leader, and a perfect instrument for God's plans for the society of his century. Several weeks later, Bernard, the Cistercian abbot of Clairvaux, met William of Champeaux, bishop of Châlons, for the first time; William, who conferred the abbatial blessing on him, was to play a very important part in his life.

From this moment, Bernard's prodigious life, which was to swing constantly between mystical contemplation and action carried at times to its uttermost limits, was marked with the sign of a twofold, and dramatic, contradiction.

To fulfil the task entrusted to Bernard would have needed, humanly speaking, a colossus. But Bernard was frail, and very soon an acute gastric illness grew into a permanent affliction, aggravated by austerities carried to excess, and which he finally had to moderate both for his own sake and for the sake of his monks. He struggled heroically against this cruel and insidious illness, and wore himself out by doing so: within a few years, the bloom of his youth faded, and the handsome Bernard of Fontaines was left only with the beauty of his soul, from which his features, emaciated by fasting and by insomnia, drew their radiance.

The other torture he underwent—and he suffered cruelly from it, only this time it was in his heart—was that he was forced to tear himself away from the silence and the darkness of the cloister before he had exhausted its delights, and to tramp the highways in order to carry out his great mission. It was then that the dramatic story of Bernard, the abbot of Clairvaux, and the guide and judge of Christendom, in the name of Christ and for his glory, began, and it was only to end at the gates of death.

All that we have to do here is to flick through the annals of the century on which the saint impressed his seal—which was the Gospel taught, explained and lived for the edification of princes and people, for the salvation of the Church and for the kingdom of God.

At first, his field of action seemed to be limited to the monastic life and, more particularly, to the affairs of his own Order. He began by founding, from 1118 to 1121, the three first daughter houses of Clairvaux: Trois-Fontaines, Fontenay and Foigny. From 1124, wherever he went, his reputation as a worker of miracles preceded him: in that year, he had healed a boy at Château-Landon of the ulcer which was gnawing at him, and, from that moment, he was constantly to multiply miracles which won the hearts of the crowds at every stage of his journey. The following year, we find him at Grenoble, at the Grande-Chartreuse, and at the synod of Langres.

From 1128—the year in which Reigny, the fifth of Clairvaux' daughter abbeys, was founded—it has been noted that Bernard was out of his monastery for approximately one month in three. That same year, he was present at the Council of Troyes, at which he was secretary and gave the Templars—a new order of monk-soldiers—their charter. In 1129, he sent men to Ourscamps, his sixth daughter house, brought about the condemnation, by the same Council of Troyes, of the bishop of Verdun, who had been convicted of simony, and upheld Stephen of Senlis, bishop of Paris, and Henri le Sanglier, archbishop of Sens, against King Louis VI and Pope Honorius II.

To those who were surprised or irritated by his interventions in the politico-religious disputes in which he was asked to arbitrate, Bernard retorted warmly and somewhat tartly: "God's affairs are my affairs; nothing which concerns him is foreign to me."

1130 was the terrible year in which the schism of Anacletus began to rage. Honorius II died on February 11th. On February 14th, two rival colleges of cardinals raised Gregory of St Angelo and Peter Pierleone to the supreme pontificate. Thus, the Church had two popes in this hour of extreme confusion—Innocent II and Anacletus II. It was necessary to choose between them. And it was Bernard who made the choice at the Council of Étampes which Louis VI had convoked in August: he chose the worthier of the two, in the person of Innocent II. The pope, who was not very safe in Rome, asked France, which had recognized him as the legitimate successor to Peter, for shelter. At Cluny, he received the homage of the Capetian king, which was brought to him by Suger. Several weeks before this, in the middle of October, Bernard, supported by Norbert, the archbishop of Magdeburg, had Innocent II acclaimed by King Lothair and the clergy of Germany in the Diet of Wurzburg. In November, Bernard was in Saint-Benoît-sur-Loire where the meeting of the pope and of the French king took place, after the Council of Clermont had condemned Anacletus II. At the end of the year, Bernard, whose hand had set the tiara more firmly on the fragile head of Innocent, conferred with King Henry of England, and rallied him to the support of the lawful pontiff.

From that moment, Bernard was torn away from the life of contemplation which he had chosen, and which he was henceforth only to taste at increasingly rare intervals; he was snowed under by activity, whose tyranny he had to endure: henceforward, nothing of any importance would be accomplished or given up without Bernard proving to be the driving force, or the brake, in it, and without his leaving on it the stamp of his genius.

From January 13th to January 17th, 1131, he was at Chartres when Innocent received the homage of Henry I of England. On Janury 19th and 20th, he was present to see the pope consecrate the abbatial church of Morigny, and there he rubbed shoulders with Abelard. Several weeks later, after visiting Provins, Châlons, Jouarre, Saint-Quentin and Cambrai with the pontifical court, he had his first theological duel with the famous master of Sainte-Geneviève in the convent of the Paraclete, where Heloïse was the abbess. On March 22nd, which was the third Sunday in Lent, King Lothair, surrounded by German princes, twenty-five archbishops and bishops, and fifty-three abbots from the religious Orders, greeted Innocent II and his retinue at Liège. During this particular interview politics threatened to do its destructive work: the monarch was attempting to exploit the still difficult position in which the pope found himself in order to force him to abolish the Concordat of Worms, so that he could obtain the right of investiture by pastoral staff and ring which Henry V had renounced. The bishops of Germany did not say a word. Then Bernard threw himself into the discussion, and forced Lothair to withdraw, thus saving the Church from the yoke of the temporal power. He even obtained from the king a promise that he would mobilize the princes who were present for an expedition against Anacletus.

At Easter, Innocent II was at Saint-Denis and at Paris. But Bernard had left him to return to Clairvaux: after all, did he not owe some of his time, in spite of everything, to his abbey? During this year 1131, he found time to provide his abbey with three more daughter houses: Cherlieu, Bonmont and Eberbach. After a few weeks, he left Clairvaux once again in order not to miss the second meeting between the pope and the king of England, which took place in Rouen at the beginning of May; there the king renewed the oath, which he had made at Chartres, to take up arms against Anacletus, who was still master of Rome. Then summer came. Innocent and his wandering cardinals spent it at Auxerre, and visited Bernard at home in Clairvaux, where the Roman court had all the leisure it needed to meditate on the lofty spiritual benefits of the monastic practices of poverty, chastity, obedience and stability.

The following year was to be more tranquil; Bernard only carried out one political act in the service of the Church during the course of that year, although this was an important one: it was his expedition to Poitiers, where the count, William X of Aquitaine, had taken up Anacletus' cause. William gave way before Bernard; but when, escaping from his influence, he came once more under the influence of the bishop of Angoulême, who was a fiery supporter of the antipope, Bernard roused the suffragans of Limoges, Poitiers, Périgueux and Saintes against the prelate, who had usurped the archiepiscopal see of Bordeaux; Bernard mobilized them against the schism, which was not to have the last word in Aquitaine or, in fact, anywhere else.

Apart from this—and while Innocent II and his retinue, who were at Cluny, at the beginning of February, were able to compare the magnificence of the Cluniac life with the unadorned austerity of Clairvaux, so much nearer St Benedict's ideal—Bernard used the year 1132 to provide the abbey, of which he was henceforward to be the head famous throughout Europe, with its tenth, eleventh, twelfth and thirteenth daughter houses—Longpont, Rievaulx, Vancelles and Moreruela, which was the first Cistercian foundation in Spain.

In the spring of 1132 the pope returned to Italy, where he prepared to lead the attack against his rival. As early as January 1133, he called for Bernard, who crossed the Alps and joined him in Pisa. The immediate task was to bring the dispute, in which Pisa and Genoa were exhausting themselves, to an end. Bernard was given the mission of suggesting to the Genoese that Innocent II should arbitrate between them. His plea was heard—for who could refuse to listen to his voice?—and his diplomacy was so effective that the two hostile cities, after signing the peace treaty at Corneto, joined in alliance against Roger of Sicily and the supporters of Anacletus.

At this point, Lothair, who had crossed into Tuscany with his army, joined Innocent at Viterbo. But he did not want to fight: he preferred to have the twofold Roman election annulled. Bernard opposed this violently: Innocent II was pope, and pope he should remain. On April 30th, pontiff, king and monk made their entry into Rome. At the beginning of June, Lothair received the imperial crown at St John Lateran. One month later, Bernard returned to France, where the pope wished him to arbitrate in a dispute brought about by the election of the new archbishop of Tours. As usual, his decision was a bold one, and he pronounced Hugh II of La Ferté to be the rightful contestant; his rival, Philip, submitted. The year ended for Bernard with the Council of Jouarre, and there he pronounced an exemplary indictment of the murderers of Thomas, the prior of Saint-Victor.

Henceforward, we shall have to choose from among the constantly increasing activities, many of them of capital importance, which filled the last twenty years of the life of Bernard of Clairvaux, the masterly instrument of the Church of Christ in her dealings with the princes of Christendom, the Catholic clergy and medieval society, whose faces had all been modelled by the saint.

We may simply remember, then, that from 1134 to 1146—the year in which we met him, at the beginning of these political, religious and social annals, at the diet of Spires—that Bernard was in turn the most active agent in the Diet of Bamberg and in the Council of Pisa (1135), in the solution to the conflict between Innocent and Lothair over the abbey of Monte Cassino and over the negotiations between the papacy and Roger of Sicily (1137), in the submission of Victor IV (elected to oppose Innocent on the death of Anacletus) which marked the end of the schism (1138), in the defeat of Abelard at the council of Sens, where his errors were condemned (1140), in the bringing to an end of the disputes between Arnold of Neuville, bishop of Lisieux, and the count of Anjou, Geoffrey Plantagenet (1141), in the settlement of the conflict between King Louis VII and Count Thibaut of Champagne (1143), in the strengthening of Eugenius III, a former monk of Clairvaux, on the throne of St Peter, and in the destruction of the heresy spread in Languedoc by Peter de Bruys (1145).

During this period, Bernard, fleeing from popular acclaim, had twice refused to allow himself to be made an archbishop, first of all in Milan, and then in Rheims; he preferred to multiply his monastic foundations, asserting by that fact that the religious life provided the basis for the disciplines which he wished to impose on the society of his time: in 1132, Clairvaux had thirteen daughter houses; at the end of 1145, she had forty-six.

The year 1146 opened on the most famous of all of Bernard's enterprises. He persuaded Louis VII to take up arms in order to free Jerusalem. In his turn, Eugenius III yielded to his pleas, and, on March 31st, published the Bull *Universis fidelibus Dei*, which set the second crusade in motion. On March 31st, Bernard was at Vézelay with the king of France, and there he gave the speech which alone was enough to ensure his fame. On May 1st, he could write to the pope:

> You gave the command, and I obeyed; it was the authority of the one who commanded that made my obedience fruitful. I opened my mouth, I spoke, and immediately crusaders multiplied beyond limit. Villages and towns are deserted. It would be difficult to find one man for every seven women. Everywhere, all that can be seen are widows whose husbands are still alive.

He took to the road, and, indefatigable, made his voice heard in Toul, Arras, Saint-Omer, Ypres, Bruges, Mainz, Worms, Frankfurt, Fribourg, Basle, Schaffouse, Constance, Zurich, Strasbourg and finally Spires.

It was here that Conrad III was crowned an emperor. Once the ceremony was over, Bernard mounted the pulpit and urged him to take the cross. The monarch hesitated. Then, three days later, as Bernard was saying Mass in front of the whole court, he stopped suddenly, turned towards Conrad and warned him that God, in his tribunal, would call him to account. The emperor gave way, and was followed by the princes around him, Frederick Barbarossa among them. The next day, December 28th, 1146, the saint was almost suffocated by the crowd which had come to hear him speak and to follow him.

Bernard's journeys continued until the moment, in May and June 1147, when Conrad III and Louis VII left Bamberg and Saint-Denis for the great expedition to the Holy Land which, by Bernard's efforts, having got off to a good start, was badly led by the princes; its eventual failure made his heart bleed—he who, more than the pope himself, was henceforth to seem the real leader of Christendom.

In spite of everything, this leader, who was inspired by God, went on with his militant activity, in constant docility to the commands of the pope, who had been his disciple; although he always regarded him as Christ's sole representative on earth, he could not help criticizing him for the choice he had made when Eugenius III entrusted to him the task of arbitrating in a fresh conflict, observing, with a humility which shows how unworthy he considered himself to be of the greatness of his mission: "A fine instrument! an ant dragging a beam.... Have I ever asked my Lord to rule churches, provide for sees and nominate bishops?"

On July 8th, 1153, soon after he had signed the treaty of Constance with Frederick Barbarossa, Eugenius III died. A few weeks later, on August 20th, Bernard, worn out, followed him to the grave. In this same month, while he was in his death-agony, Clairvaux' sixty-eighth daughter house, La Peyrouse, was founded.

We might thus be tempted to believe that the century in which St Bernard lived was completely dominated by him; we might think that the monk of Clairvaux must have ruled the Church and the society of his time, bishops and leaders of religious Orders, princes and men of war, artists and philosophers, even the emperor himself, and the pope himself. In fact things were quite different; whatever Bernard of Fontaines' personal genius might have been, it seems clear that he was content, without failing in humility, as a churchman of his time, to carry within himself all through his travels, as well as his cloister of Clairvaux— to repeat the picturesque image of one of his biographers —the thought of Hildebrand, another monk whose spiritual heir he proved to be, who had lived a century before him and who had worn the tiara under the name of Gregory VII.

Bernard's deepest ideal was solitude; this was fully expressed in the inscription which still flowers today on the threshold of Cistercian abbeys—*O beata solitudo! O sola beatitudo!* If Bernard seemed—and he only seemed—to yield to the giddy whirl of political action, we can be sure that he did it solely in order to accomplish his supernatural mission, which was to fashion medieval, ecclesiastical and secular society in the Gregorian image, according to the plan of the great Tuscan pontiff, of whom it has been said that, better than Alexander and Caesar themselves, he could conceive of a great political structure in which humanity could find a home.

The threads which Bernard of Clairvaux used in order to weave the startling tapestry of his activity were the *Dictatus Papae*, promulgated in 1075 by Gregory VII, which proclaimed the sovereignty of the Roman pontiff: the Church had been founded by Christ; the pope is the universal head of the Church; he has absolute and limitless power over it, and over lay society as well; he can depose emperors; the temporal power is in all things subordinate to the spiritual power. However, if the Church, a spiritual power, is thus to rule the State, a temporal power, it is essential that she should be worthy of the task; she must be holy; and that was why Bernard of Clairvaux, even while he was fighting for the Church against the princes, roundly attacked canons, abbots and bishops when he saw them weaken or betray the Church; in his eyes, it was not enough to appeal to the Gregorian principles; the Church had to justify the rigid application of them by placing herself above all criticism and beyond all suspicion.

This rigid, even pitiless, doctrine, which formed the basis for his activity, was formulated tirelessly by St Bernard in the spoken and written word, in sermons, letters and treatises, which all make up a prodigious monument to his thought and have earned him the title of the last, in date, of the Fathers of the Church. But because he took care not to legislate in the abstract, and because it was his constant desire, at the cost of his inner peace, to remain in contact with the men of his time, he was most fully effective in the knowledge of hearts and minds: Bernard of Clairvaux was an astonishing psychologist; no matter who he was addressing, he could speak in the appropriate manner, and thus make himself understood in all circumstances by everyone.

Sometimes the language he uses is blunt. When he addresses the great, he verges on audacity, and even on temerity; but, because he was lucid, he proved to be effective, and when Bernard was speaking or writing, nobody dared to stop up his ears or to shut his eyes.

A few short examples of his style will be in place here.

To Louis VI, king of France:

> The King of heaven and earth has given you royalty on earth, and will give it to you in heaven also, provided that

you apply yourself to administering justly and wisely what you have received. This is what we hope for you, offering our prayers so that you may reign faithfully here below, and may reign happily above.

To Louis VII:

The kingdoms of the earth and the royal rights belong to the sovereign only to the extent that he conforms to God's laws and God's wishes.

To the Emperor Conrad:

Both swords, spiritual and temporal, belong to the Church, but the latter, like the former, must be drawn by the Church alone; the spiritual sword belongs to the priest; the temporal sword lies in the soldier's hand, but it cannot be used except on a sign from the priest and on command of the emperor. . . .

Let the human will strive to carry out what divine authority has ordained, and let those who have been united by custom be united by the heart also! Let them love each other, defend each other, and bear their burdens together!

To Melisande, queen of Jerusalem:

Take care not to let the pleasures of the flesh and concern for temporal glory close the entrance to the Kingdom of Heaven for you. What is the use of reigning for a few days on earth only to be deprived afterwards of the eternal kingdom? Take an interest in strangers, in the poor, and in prisoners, for it is by the intercession of victims like these that you will merit God.

To Roger, king of Sicily:

He is truly happy who listens not to the greedy, but to the needy and the poor—yes, it is true, to the poor man who asks in spite of himself, who receives with modesty, and who, by receiving in this way, glorifies his Father who is in Heaven. . . . Listen patiently to the account of their sufferings, listen, and you will suffer with them; and if you suffer with them, you will also reign with them. A king ought not to despise the thought of reigning with men like these, for the kingdom of heaven belongs to those who despise the life of the world.

To William, duke of Aquitaine:

You know that it is not in order to destroy our subjects that we rule, but to guide them. He who allows kings to reign has set us at the head of his people so that we can serve them, and not so that we can pervert them; we are the ministers of holy Church, and not her masters.

To the rich:

Those who are naked cry out; those who go hungry cry out; and they say: What use are all those changes of clothing, spread on poles or folded away in wardrobes, to us, suffering miserably from cold and hunger as we are? The wealth which you are spending so prodigally belongs to us; the wealth which you are wasting uselessly has been cruelly torn from us. We, too, are creatures of God; we, too, have been redeemed by the Blood of Christ. So we are your brothers. Think of what you are guilty when you feed your eyes with the portion which belongs to a brother. Your life is spent in wasting what is superfluous. . . .

It is certain that you will one day lose all that you possess on earth, apart from what you have succeeded in having carried in advance to heaven by the hands of the poor. So lay up treasure for yourselves in heaven, where there is no moth to destroy it, nor thieves to break in and steal it, and where even your lord himself cannot take anything away from you. If you want messengers, you have not one, but several, at your door who will faithfully deliver what you wish to be carried.

To effeminate lords:

Are those the insignia of soldiers, or are they the adornments of women? Can it be that the enemy's sword will fear gold, spare precious stones and not be able to pierce silks?

To women:

Silk, purple and the splendour borrowed from dyes may all possess beauty, but they cannot transmit it. Everything like this that we apply to our bodies is mere show, and does not last once we have taken it off. The beauty which we put on with our clothes disappears with them; it belongs to the clothing and not to the woman who is wearing it.

To the idle:

There is pleasure, it is said, in making conversation in order to pass the time and to waste an hour! What is that? This hour which the mercy of God gives you in order to do penance, to obtain pardon, to acquire grace, and to merit the glory of our promised heaven! And this time which you could use in order to make yourself pleasing to the divine power, to hasten towards the company of the angels, to sigh over the inheritance which we have lost, to stir up your lazy will, and to weep over your sins! Would to God that it was only the time of a man's earthly life that he lost in empty conversation! But, too often, it is eternal life that he loses in his wretchedness.

To those who opposed Christian marriage:

One has to be a beast not to see that to condemn a just marriage is to loosen the reins for all sorts of impurities. Take honourable marriage and a spotless bed from the Church, and you will fill her with concubinage, incest and foul behaviour. So choose whether you are going to fill heaven with monsters who practise these things, or whether you are going to limit the number of the elect only to those who are continent. But continence is a rare thing on earth. Are we to believe that the Saviour annihilated himself solely for continence? How could we all have received the fullness of his grace if only the continent have a share in it? And what right have we to limit God's power in this way?

To parents angered by their children's religious vocations:

If God takes your son to be his own son, what will you yourselves lose, and what can he lose himself? From being rich, he becomes even richer, from being noble, even nobler, from being famous, even more famous, and, what is of greater importance still, from being a sinner, he is transformed into a saint. If you love him, rejoice, for he is going towards his Father, and what a Father! He is going towards God, but you are not losing him.

To the people of Rome who had risen against the pope:

Why do you, with a fury as intolerable as it is unreasonable, provoke the King of earth and the Lord of heaven, by rising with sacrilegious audacity against the holy, apostolic See, which is given extraordinary glory by its divine privileges, and by trying to lessen its prerogatives, whereas, if it had proved necessary, you should have defended it alone against all?

To the people of Milan in revolt:

By a special privilege, fullness of power over all the Churches of the world has been given to the Holy See. Anyone who resists its power is resisting the order willed by God.

If anyone tells you that you must obey in part, and refuse obedience on other points, while you know the fullness of apostolic authority and the universality of its powers, do you not think that the man who speaks in this way has either allowed himself to be seduced, or wishes to seduce others? So do what I tell you, for I certainly am not a seducer.

To Cistercian abbots:

Our lot is abjection, humility, voluntary poverty, obedience, peace and joy in the Holy Spirit. Our lot is to be in subjection to a superior, under an abbot and under a discipline; our lot is to practise silence, fasting, vigils and manual work, and, above all else, to follow the royal road which is charity, to progress in it day by day, and to persevere in it until our last hour.

To Cluniac abbots:

This is permissible for bishops; they have duties both to the wise and the stupid, and so they try to stir up the devotion of uncultured people through material ornaments, since they cannot do it sufficiently through spiritual ones. But as for us, who have left all that is precious and pleasurable in the world for the love of Jesus Christ, and who have looked upon all that is splendid, charming, sweetly scented, delightful, pleasurable and flattering to the senses as dung, in order to win Jesus Christ, whose devotion, may I ask, are we trying to arouse? What fruit do we wish to draw from all these things? Is it the admiration of the foolish, or the satisfaction of the simple?

May I be called a liar, if I have not seen an abbot with sixty horses and more in his train. If you saw them pass, you would think that they were lords of castles instead of shepherds of monasteries, and governors of provinces instead of guides of souls.

To bishops:

If your office does not allow you to be poor, at least let your conduct show that you love the poor; for it is not poverty, but the love of poverty, which is a virtue.... I urge you to befriend the poor, but to befriend poverty even more; anyone who loves the poor has set his foot on the way, but the man who loves poverty has reached the goal; the love of the poor will make you the friend of kings, but the love of poverty will make you a king yourself.

If you have not lost your reason completely, if you still have a heart to feel and eyes to see, stop chasing after things which it is only a misfortune to attain.

To the pope:

You are not only the pastor of all the sheep; you are also the pastor of all the pastors; you are the one vicar of Christ.

In this way, the Church acted, in her dealings with princes and peoples, and with herself, through St Bernard.

CHAPTER IV

A POOR MAN NAMED FRANCIS

The son of Bernardone, a wealthy cloth merchant, faced his father in the middle of the great square of Assisi; near them, surrounded by a great crowd of people, was Guido, the bishop. With unhurried movements, and with a look of perfect simplicity on his face, Francis took off his rich man's clothes, and threw them down one by one, together with his purse, at the feet of the man responsible for his birth. All that he kept was his shirt. Over this, he put on a mended piece of sackcloth, in which he had made a hole for his head; he fastened it at his waist with a piece of cord; and then, barefoot, he set off.

This was the one moment, since that time on Golgotha when the Roman soldiers, before nailing Jesus the Nazarene to the cross, removed his seamless garment, when a Christian tried to be like Christ as completely as possible.

In spite of this, the most important thing was what was to come. Bishop Guido, from whom Bernardone had demanded the return of Francis to his home, refused to hand him back and return him to the world, and took him under his protection. By this act, the Church chose to act through Francis of Assisi, a man wedded to Lady Poverty, in order to fight against Money, the master of the world, and an open wound in the hearts of men. From that moment, all that the Christians of the thirteenth century had to do was to look at the life of the man who was henceforward to be called the Poverello, and all that the Christians of ages to come had to do was to meditate on the words which fell from his lips, and which were preserved through the devotion of those who strove to imitate him, in order to know how a disciple of Christ ought to behave if he wishes to resemble Jesus his master.

There was nothing in his background which predisposed Francis Bernardone to become such as he now was. This was the work of God within him, the action of grace, stamped with a profound mystery, as had happened, before him, to Paul of Tarsus, the Pharisee who butchered the Christians, to Augustine of Tagaste, a rhetorician and a debauchee and to Bernard of Fontaines, a knight seemingly destined to the brutal game of war, and, after him, to Ignatius of Loyola, who was a Reiter and a libertine right up to the siege of Pamplona. Francis was a fop, applauded and followed by the golden youth of his town. Up to the moment when the bolt of divine love, which was to turn them into saviours of souls, fell on them, all five of these men were in the process of losing their own souls; day by day, they were damning themselves.

At twenty years of age, Francis was the golden fruit of the Umbrian earth, which had ripened beneath the Italian sun on a middle-class tree fed with rich manure. He flung away his father's hard cash in prodigious handfuls, used and abused pleasures and dragged in his train a court which, fascinated by his expensive living, shamelessly pillaged his purse which was open to all. He made war, too, with varied fortunes. Perugia kept him in her prisons. When he returned, he was already a different person; God had visited him while he had been a captive, and Francis had felt his approach. Then he began to change his ways, shunned the joys of Assisi, and loved to withdraw alone into the grottoes of Mount Subasio. One day, he met a leper on the road, and committed his first act of folly; he approached the impure creature, took him in his arms, and kissed him on the mouth. When he went on a pilgrimage to Rome, he begged in the streets, at the corners of the cool squares, in order to humiliate himself. When he returned to his own city of Assisi, he spent his days in prayer, wrapped in darkness and silence, beneath the vaults of San Damiano; and it was there that Jesus, in his turn, spoke to him for the first time:

"Francis," he said, "rebuild my house, for it is crumbling away."

Francis, not understanding what his Master wanted of him, began to restore the old dilapidated sanctuaries of Assisi; he had not yet begun to restore, as the Lord had meant, the cracked building of his Church.

Another day—this again happened in San Damiano— he was enlightened during Mass by the passage in the Gospel where Christ tells his disciples to go and preach the kingdom of God; so Francis ran, and awoke the echoes in the streets and squares of Assisi with his voice; friends began to attach themselves to him; Francis counted them; when they were twelve in all, he left with them for Rome, and came to offer himself to Pope Innocent III in the Lateran palace.

At the request of Bishop Guido and of Cardinal Giovanni Colonna, the pontiff welcomed him and listened to him; in wonderment, he discovered what sort of surprising creature he had before him, and did not hesitate for a second; the Church was to act through Francis; the twelve would become thousands, millions, through the centuries to come, for the Order of Friars Minor had just been born, and it would never stop growing and flourishing in the world by means of those who, beneath the brown homespun, would choose to take up the cross with Jesus, to bear it on their backs and to follow him.

In this way, there began the most picturesque, inspiring
and rich adventure, in which, for the last seven centuries,
God has wished to see his chosen ones take part. St
Francis' Order may have been split up, made mistakes or
contradicted itself; but Francis himself, the Poverello, is
still living among his sons, and he continues to teach men
the lesson of Christ re-found.

This lesson is addressed, first of all, to the brothers. He
has left them the Rule for their inheritance, after com-
menting on it to them in unforgettable words:

> You must know that the Rule is the book of life, the
> hope of salvation, the marrow of the Gospel, the way of
> perfection, the key to Heaven, the covenant of the eternal
> alliance. . . .
>
> In the name of the Lord, go out two by two, and go
> forward on the roads bearing yourselves modestly; above
> all, observe silence and, from morning until Terce, speak
> with God in your hearts, avoiding the exchange of idle or
> useless words with one another. As you travel, your attitude
> ought to be as religious as when you are in a hermitage or
> in a cell; wherever we are, we carry our cell with us; Brother
> body is our cell, and our soul is the hermit who dwells in its
> shelter in order to meditate and to adore God. . . .
>
> Preach peace and repentance to men so that their sins
> should be forgiven them; be patient under trials, sure of
> accomplishing God's plans and of realizing his promises.
> Reply humbly to those who ask you questions. Bless those
> who persecute you, and thank those who heap insults and
> calumnies on you, for an eternal kingdom is awaiting
> you. . . .
>
> Do not be afraid. In a short while, many learned men and
> many noble men will come to you; with you they will teach
> kings, princes and a great host of peoples. Great numbers
> will be converted to God, who will multiply his family
> throughout the world. . . .
>
> Do not be afraid to appear little and ignorant; do not
> fear to preach repentance in a simple manner. Set your

confidence in God, who has conquered the world. Retain a firm hope in him. Believe that the Spirit will speak in you and through you, in order to urge men to conversion. Among men, you will find some who are faithful and who wish you well, who will give a joyful welcome both to you yourselves and to the things you say; others, who will be numerous, will prove to be rebellious, infatuated as they are with themselves, with blasphemy and insults on their lips, and will reject you. So you must dispose your hearts to suffer everything patiently and humbly. . . .

You must know, brethren, that poverty is our own special road to salvation, in that it is a leaven of humility and a source of perfection. Its fruits are many, but hidden; poverty is the treasure hidden in the field of which Scripture speaks: to purchase it, we have to sell all the field. . . .

We, who have renounced everything, must take care not to lose the kingdom of heaven over trifles; if we find any money, we must pay no more attention to it than to the dust which we tread under our feet. . . .

The further the brethren depart from poverty, the more will the world leave them; but if they remain attached to Poverty, my Lady, the world will feed them, for they have been given to the world for its salvation. . . .

My very dear brethren, do not let us feel any shame at begging, my little children. The Lord made himself poor for our sakes; following his example, we have chosen the way of true poverty, which was also the way of his most holy Mother. This is the inheritance which our Lord Jesus Christ gained for us, and which he has left to us and to all who have decided, like us, to live in holy poverty. . . .

When you see a poor man, you must think of him in whose name this poor man comes—you must think of Christ who wished to clothe himself in our poverty and weakness. The weakness and poverty of this man form a mirror in which, with devotion, our eyes can make out the weakness and the poverty with which our Lord Jesus Christ clothed himself bodily for the salvation of mankind. . . .

I want all the brethren to work and to give themselves humbly to honest tasks, so that they will be less of a burden

on other men, and so that their tongues and hearts will not
go astray into idleness. Those who do not know how to do
anything must learn. . . .

Dearly beloved brethren, at the first word, obey the
commands given to you. Do not object that they are impossible; for, if I were to command you to do something
which is beyond your powers, obedience would itself be
strong enough to make you strong enough too. . . .

If any among you wishes to be great, he must make himself the servant of all; if any wishes to be the first of all, he
must become the slave of all. . . .

When you preach peace, peace is on your lips; but you
must also, and even more, have it in your hearts. No one
must be roused to anger or to scandal because of you; all,
seeing your meekness, should feel moved to goodness and
to concord; for we are invited to care for the wounded, to
unite those who have been separated and to bring back to
the truth those who have strayed into error. Those who may
seem to us to belong to the Devil, will one day be the
disciples of Jesus Christ. . . .

I beg my brothers who are sick not to become angry with
God, and not to disturb themselves or their brethren either;
they must not ask for medicines too insistently; they must
not have any excessive desire for this flesh of ours, destined
for an early death, to be healed; instead, they are to be
grateful for everything, and want to be as God wants them,
for God, who has predestined them into eternal life, is
preparing them for it with the lash of infirmity, as he himself has said: Those whom I love, I test and correct. . . .

My dear brethren, little children, do not allow my in-
firmities to disgust you or cause you suffering. Both in this
world and in the world to come, the Lord will restore to
you, for me his base servant, all the merit that you would
have reaped for the work which you cannot do now because
of the lavish care that you bestow on me. In this way, you
are acquiring greater merit than those who dedicate themselves completely to religion and to their brethren. Do even
more, and say to me: We are spending this for you, but it
is the Lord who is our debtor. . . .

I want the brethren to study Scripture, on condition that they should follow the example of Christ, who prayed more than he read, and not neglect prayer, and that they should apply themselves less to learning how to speak than to putting what they have learnt into practice and to urging others to practise the same things. I want the brothers to be disciples of the Gospel and to grow in knowledge of truth, in order thus to grow in the purest simplicity. . . .

Others have worked and taught according to what they knew; but I have given salvation through your merits, and you will receive the reward for this, that eternal kingdom which has been conquered by your humility, your simplicity and the ardour of your prayers and tears. . . .

Dear brothers, thank our Lord Jesus Christ for having been willing to dispense the heavenly treasures of heaven through the mouths of simple men. . . .

Lord, I leave this family to you. . . . The brothers have their Rule. . . . They have sworn to keep it. . . . From the moment when the brothers know what it is that they have to do, and what it is that they have to avoid, all that there remains for me to do is to teach them by what I do myself: it was for this that I was given to them, both during my lifetime and after my death. . . .

Woe to those who trust to the mere appearances of the religious life, who pride themselves on their knowledge and who remain idle; those, I mean, who do not practise the works of virtue by the cross, by penance and by the following of the Gospel to which they are bound by their profession, in all purity and simplicity. They will not be able to put up a fight against temptation, which is permitted so that the elect might be tested. But those who, when put to the test, prove to be strong, will receive the crown of life. . . .

Brothers, the Lord called me by a humble voice, and he has led me along a simple road. . . . The Lord told me that he wanted me to be a fool in the world; and the only road along which God wished to lead us, was the road of that sort of wisdom. . . .

Jesus, my Lord, you instituted this religion of the brothers in order to strengthen the faith of men, and to accomplish

the mystery of your Gospel thanks to them. . . . So let those
who, through their bad example, destroy what you have
already built, and what you continue to build, by means of
the holy brothers of this Order, be cursed by you, most holy
Lord, by the whole court of heaven, and by me, poor little
creature that I am. . . .

In memory of my blessing and of my testament, let them
always love one another, and be full of consideration for
each other; let them always love and honour our lady
Poverty; let them be faithful and submissive to the bishops
and priests of our holy mother the Church. . . .

Farewell, all my sons. Grow in the fear of the Lord and
constantly dwell in him, for a great temptation hangs over
you and the time of tribulation is near. Happy are those
who persevere in their works! The scandals which will come
will drive some away. But I am hastening towards the Lord
my God.

When Innocent III had given him permission to found
a new spiritual family, Francis had not forgotten—and he
would never forget—that his real mission was to speak
and act, not only, and not even primarily, for his Friars
Minor, who would be the source of many disappoint-
ments and a great deal of sadness for him, but for
all men, and especially for the most sinful and the most
unfortunate; this was a universal mission which was also
the mission of the Church; and it was a sublime task
which the Poverello still fulfils today and will continue to
fulfil to the end of time.

Because this little brother Francis knew himself well, he
knew from which direction sin first takes hold of human
nature, and the teaching he gives is aimed at each of us
in our most intimate weakness, which is the ceaseless
battle between the soul and the body from which the body
too often emerges victorious. We can hear the warning:

Man's worst enemy is his flesh. It cannot keep any
memory of the past, in order to repent of it, nor can it

foresee the future, in order to take precautions against it; its sole concern is to misuse the present. Even more serious, it turns gifts belonging to the soul, and not to itself, to its own credit, and glories in them. It welcomes praise directed to the virtues of the soul, and the admiration which is aroused by vigils and prayer. The flesh leaves nothing for the soul; it even goes further, and causes the soul to weep. . . .

When the soul is deprived of spiritual joy, what is left for the body? The flesh returns to its pleasures, bestial degradation is justified by necessity, and conscience is replaced by the carnal sense. . . . How can we satisfy the needs of the body without succumbing to the lure of sensuality?

But Francis forbids us to despise and torture this flesh which is both demanding and wretched; it has its own part to play; it is enough for us to keep a close watch over it, without weakness or cruelty:

The servant of God must obey with moderation the needs of the body in food and sleep and everything else. Brother body must never be allowed to protest: "It is impossible for me to remain on my feet, to pray, to rejoice in adversity and to do any good works, for you refuse to satisfy my needs". . . .

It is through the body that the devil has a hold on us. Francis testifies to this with a great humility, in the light of his own experience; he also explains to us why and how we are tempted, with God's permission:

Why have devils attacked me in this way? Why has the Lord granted them the power to harm me, if not because they are his policemen? Just as society sends policemen to punish those who flout it, so God punishes those whom he loves through the intervention of his own policemen—the devils—who have been appointed to fill this office. . . .

Tonight, I was prevented from sleeping, and I could not persevere in prayer once I had got up. My head ached, my knees felt weak beneath me, and the whole of my body was shaken with trembling, as if I had eaten a darnel loaf. It seemed to me that the devil was hidden in the feather pillow on which my head lay; take it away—I do not wish to have the devil beneath my head. As I was reciting Compline yesterday evening, I saw that the devil was prowling in my cell.... He is an extremely astute and subtle creature. God, in the mercy of his grace, does not allow him to harm my soul; but then he denies one of the needs of my body by denying me sleep; he prevents me from standing up to pray, in order to deprive me of devotion, to take away the joy of my heart and to force me to curse my weakness.... Do everything you wish to me, cunning spirit; the only power that you possess is the power which God's hand gives you, and I am ready to suffer joyfully all that it pleases him to inflict on me.

Because he knew himself to be so vulnerable and so weak, Francis developed a heart-rending humility; he had no illusions about himself, and he refused to delude others, proclaiming his unworthiness to them:

You come to me with great devotion and you imagine that I am a saint; but I confess before God and before you, that I ate bacon during Lent ...

I want to live in the sight of God as I would wish to be known by men; if I thought that I was a saint, while I did not live in a saintly manner, I should be nothing more than a hypocrite ...

If you want me to keep this fur beneath my tunic, put another one on top, so that everyone will know that I have one underneath as well ...

I believe that I am the greatest of sinners; if God had shown the same mercy to a criminal as he has shown to me, that criminal would have been ten times as holy as I am ...

In order to carry out the marvellous work which he planned to accomplish, God was not able to find a viler creature than myself in the whole world; it was for this reason that he chose me. For God uses fools here on earth in order to confound the wise; he uses the unknown, the despised and the sick to confound famous and powerful men; thus, no creature can glory in itself, but only in the Lord . . .

Brother Francis, you have committed so many sins in your life that you deserve hell . . . Lord, King of Heaven and earth, I have committed so many sins against you that I deserve to be damned to the core of my being. . . . Why do you not answer, Brother Leo, as I taught you to do? In the name of holy obedience, I command you to reply to me in the way that I tell you. I shall say: Wretched Francis, do you hope that the Lord will have pity on you, you who have sinned in this way against the Father of all mercy? And you, little sheep, will reply: You are in no way worthy of obtaining mercy.

It was surely very natural that, in his profound humility, Francis should have turned towards the humblest of God's creatures, and should talk familiarly to them. So he spoke to animals, so much better than men in his clear-sighted view:

Brother birds, God loves you and you must praise him always and everywhere, for allowing you to fly freely in every place, for your clothes, which are doubly and triply lined and which are coloured and embroidered, for the food which is constantly offered to you without your having to work for it, for the song with which the Creator fills your throats, for your numbers which grow with his blessing, for your offspring which he will preserve from the flood in the Ark, and for the air which he has given you for your kingdom. You do not sow, neither do you reap: God feeds you; he gives you spring water to drink; he gives you mountains and hills for shelter, and rocks and thickets where you can build your nests; without teaching you to spin and sew, he clothes you, with your children. . . . He must surely love you very much if he showers you with as many gifts as these. And so, brother birds, do not be ungrateful, but go on ceaselessly praising the Creator. . . .

Sister lark wears a hood like a religious; she is a humble bird, seeking for her seeds. along the highways, if she finds some mingled with dung, she is not repelled, but picks them out and eats them. She praises the Lord during her flight in the heavenly regions, just like every religious who takes care to despise the things of the earth, in order to live completely in heaven. Her habit, her plumage, is like the earth, an example for religious for whom a dead colour like the soil, and not luxurious habits and bright colours, is suitable. . . .

Simple, chaste, innocent doves, why do you allow your-selves to be caught? I shall save you from death, and build you nests where you will be able to reproduce, in accordance with the will of the Creator, who commands you to multiply. . . .

Do you see that gentle sheep over there, trotting among the goats. I tell you that it was in this way that the Lord walked among the Pharisees and the chief priests. For love of him, have pity like me on that sheep; buy it, and remove it from the company of the goats. . . .

Come here, brother wolf. In the name of Christ, I com-mand you not to harm me or anyone else. Brother wolf, you have done a great deal of damage in this land; you have committed abominable crimes, pitilessly killing the creatures of God, animals as well as the men who are made in God's image; this is a crime which explains why you are hated. . . . For all these things, what you deserve, thief and murderer, is an exemplary death. Everyone rightly murmurs and cries out against you. You are the enemy of all. But I wish to establish peace between men and you. Do not harm them any more, and they will forget your crimes; in future, no one, neither man nor dog, will persecute you. If you wish to make peace, brother wolf, I promise, in the name of the town, to have everything you need brought out to you; so you will never again go hungry; I know, you see, that all the evil you did came from the fact that you were hungry. The only condition, in return for the favour which I shall obtain for you, is that you should promise me not to harm man or beast any more. Do you promise. . .?

Francis Bernardone of Assisi was a poet, and the equal of the greatest poets. If he had been content to write verse, he would have known glory such as man can give; but he preferred to live for the glory of God, for he knew the ridiculous worth of an earthly life of which only human genius survives; and he knew, too, the true, profound meaning of death.

In the face of death, he did not turn away his gaze or tremble:

"Brother doctor," he said, "do not be afraid to tell me that death is coming. For me, it will be the gateway to life." In order to give this caller a fitting welcome, he ordered: "When you feel that my last moments have come, lay me out naked on the ground, as you saw me three days ago; when I am dead, let me lie like this for as long as it takes to travel a mile without hurrying."

Then death was there. He greeted it: "Sister death, welcome!"

If we are to understand the lesson which the Poverello has to teach us, we must keep before us the picture of his hands and feet pierced like those of Christ; by impressing his stigmata on him, Jesus wished to show man that none of them had resembled him more closely than little brother Francis. It is also as well for us not to forget the avowal which came from the lips of Francis: "I know the poor and crucified Christ, and do not need to know anything more."

In this way, against pride and money, the destroyers of the soul, the Church acted through St Francis.

CHAPTER V

LOYOLA, THE SOLDIER
OF CHRIST

On May 20th, 1521, the French troops of the count of
Foix were besieging the citadel of Pamplona, in Navarre.
The Spanish captain, Iñigo de Loyola, who was defending
the position for the duke of Najera, the viceroy whom
Ferdinand of Aragon had nominated for the province, was
brought down by a cannon ball, fired from the French
lines, and both his legs were broken. Deprived of the man
who was its driving force, the garrison surrendered. At
this same moment, another inviolable fortress, occupied
by other invincible troops, and led by a similar inflexible
leader, was on the point of being set up in the skies of the
Church, and would protect her, at the victorious level of
the spirit, against all the attacks mounted by her enemies.

Captain Iñigo, however, was nothing more than a foppish
soldier, a swaggerer, a frequenter of bed-chambers, a
Basque, who said his prayers and who was fiercely concerned with his honour, like all the men of his race, but
who could only, in the end, behave in an arrogant, cynical
and voluptuous way—a man far from sanctity, and even
from virtue, who would have deserved to be despised if it
had not been for his courage.

And he did show that he had courage, and to spare,
under the clumsy handling first of the French, and then of

the Spanish surgeons, who were quick to inflict tortures
on him. After his right leg had been summarily patched up,
he was laid on a stretcher and brought back to Guipuzcoa,
to the castle of his ancestors, the lords of Oñaz and Loyola.
With his badly set tibia, the road was torture for him. And
when he came safely into harbour, he was ready to be
butchered (as he himself described it). In an attempt to
lengthen his shortened limb, his executioners invented a
clever apparatus which used cords, planks and heavy
weights. The suffering this caused Iñigo brought him to the
point of screaming. He contented himself with clenching his
fists; but thought that he would faint from anguish when
he realized that he would always be a cripple: how would
it be possible for him in this state once more to go and
court his princess, the gentle infanta Catalina, whose love-
filled youth was drooping as she spent it by the side of
her mother, the mad queen Joan? Iñigo's career as a
gallant and a warrior had ended. All that Ignatius—as he
had decided to call himself in future—could do was to
choose a higher love and a more glorious fight—the love
with which man burns for God and the fight which he
wages for him. The well-aimed cannon ball at Pamplona
had opened a breach in the hidalgo's vain and perverted
heart, through which grace and heroic virtues were to enter
and turn a wretched sinner into a saint.

The second stage along the road on which his wonderful
destiny was to make him walk was Manresa—a confined
Catalan city on the banks of the Cardoner, in which he
stopped, after leaving the famous monastery of Montserrat,
and took shelter in a grotto, in God's presence alone.

Ignatius had arrived there, limping, after abandoning his
dagger and sword, and his rough breastplate and velvet
doublet at the foot of the greatly venerated statue of our
Lady of Battles in order to put on the austere garb of
pilgrims going to the Holy Land; he was already thinking

of going to Jerusalem on his wounded legs, to offer his life as a holocaust before Christ's tomb.

Ignatius of Loyola had read a great deal during the months of his martyrdom and of his immobile convalescence; naturally enough, he had begun with romances of chivalry; and then he had turned to religious books, just as he chanced to find them. The hidden genius which lay sleeping within him, and the intimate voice which the senseless bustle of the battlefield had drowned, sprang to life, and echoed in the deepest recesses of his soul, which was soon open, first to the awareness of God and then to the vision of him. He felt a new ambition dawn in his soul and beat in harmony with his renewed heart—an ambition in which the glory of arms no longer had any part, but which was dominated by the glory of God, whose knight he now dreamt of becoming. Up to this moment, had this warrior, a prisoner in a narrow and ridiculous world, any awareness of his own age and of the reality of the fight in which the Church was taking part in this first quarter of the sixteenth century, which saw Luther break with Rome and lead the attack against her? It was at this moment that what Daniel-Rops has been able to call the reawakening of the Catholic soul first took shape; on it, he writes:

> An intense spiritual ferment was producing fruit in the shape of a host of achievements in the sphere of the apostolate, charity and discipline; innumerable people of good will declared that they were ready to serve and were already supplying themselves with effective means. This reawakening of the Catholic soul, this return to a "religion once more become life", to use the expression of the Protestant Leonard, was clearly rich with promise. And it was the task of a man of genius, a mystic who was also an organizer, to synthesize all these aspirations and efforts, and so endow the new Church; this was the historical destiny of St Ignatius of Loyola.

At Manresa, where he had arrived with his scrip over his shoulder and with the badge of St James on his stick, with unkempt hair, and more than shabbily dressed, the lame man of Pamplona buried himself in the solitude and darkness of his cave—a stranger to the life of the world, and inaccessible to the commerce of men, struggling with himself and using his days and nights to seek himself, to know himself, and to impose his own law upon himself, in that conquest of self which turns the old man into a slave subjected to the inflexible will of the new man who has just broken his matrix of sin, and who rises, bearing aloft the weapons of the spirit, in order to subject each soul to the Church and the whole world to God.

The different phases of his experience, which was beyond any human measure, had been written down one by one, and from these preliminary notes, as rich as they were concise, came the little treatise known as the *Spiritual Exercises*; it was drawn up for his own private use. Before communicating the *Exercises* to those who were soon to become his disciples, Ignatius of Loyola forged the armour and the sword with which all Christians anxious to face up to the world, to evil, and to their own self, and to defeat them all, would wage the fight of the invincible knights of Christ.

If we do not know this monumental work, at least in its outlines and in its essential passages, we shall know nothing about its author—a man of genius, as well as one inspired by the Holy Spirit—or about the action carried on by the Church through him for four and a half centuries. Because Ignatius of Loyola drew the human substance of the *Spiritual Exercises* from within himself alone, he is mirrored in them in his most authentic and living reality; and the study of them teaches us how a man, no matter what sort of man he might be, by using them rationally—that is, by using them as a key fashioned to open the most hidden fortress of the soul—can, if he so wishes and if he applies himself honestly to the task, batter down the sin within him, and, by grace, live in intimate friendship with God.

The little book begins with a series of practical notes—twenty in all—which, without irreverence, can be compared to the paragraphs of the "directions for use" of some medical treatment or apparatus.

To begin, there is a definition: what are the *Exercises,* and what are they for?

> By this name of *Spiritual Exercises* is understood every method of examination of conscience, of meditation or contemplation, of vocal and mental prayer, and of doing other spiritual works, as is pointed out in what follows. For, just as strolling, walking and running are bodily exercises, so every method of preparing and disposing our souls to rid themselves of all unruly affections, and, after these have been eradicated, to seek and discover the divine will, concerning the disposition of our lives for the salvation of our souls, is called a spiritual exercise.

A little later, the way in which they have to be used, which varies from one person to another, is pointed out.

> Four weeks are taken for the following Exercises, corresponding with the four parts which make them up. The first part is the consideration and contemplation of our sins; the second is the life of our Lord Jesus Christ until Palm Sunday inclusive; the third is the passion of our Lord Jesus Christ; the fourth is the resurrection and ascension, which is followed by three methods of praying. However, this division into weeks is not to be taken to mean that each has necessarily to have seven or eight days. For, just as it happens that some are slower to find what they are looking for in the first week—that is, contrition, sorrow and tears with which to weep for their sins—so some are more diligent, and more agitated or tested by the various spirits. For this reason, it is sometimes necessary to shorten this week, and sometimes necessary to lengthen it, a practice which should also be followed in all the following weeks, always

looking for the fruit proper to the matter it contains. Even so, the Exercises will still be completed in the space of thirty days, more or less.

After this come the directions—which are astonishingly precise, for nothing must be left to chance or to improvisation in the *Exercises*—some of which are intended for those receiving the *Exercises* and others for those giving them.

It is a wonderful advantage for anyone receiving the Exercises to enter upon them wholeheartedly and with generosity towards his Creator and Lord, offering all his will and liberty to him, so that the divine Majesty should dispose of him and of all that he possesses according to his most holy will.

When the one giving the Exercises sees that the one making them is not experiencing any spiritual movement, such as consolations or desolations, in his soul . . . he must question him carefully on the Exercises, to see whether he is making them at the time laid down, and how he is making them, and he must do the same in the case of the Additions, inquiring whether he is observing them diligently; he is to demand a detailed account on all these points.

If the one giving the Exercises sees that the one receiving them is a prey to desolation and temptation, far from seeming harsh or severe towards him, he must be kind and gentle with him, giving him courage and strength for what is to follow, revealing the tricks of the enemy of human nature to him, and sparing himself nothing to bring it about that he should prepare and dispose himself for future consolations.

There follow other subtle directions, which show that Loyola was a master tactician in pedagogy, as well as a fighter used to the wiles of the enemy, that is, of the Devil.

It is to the advantage of the one making the Exercises not to know, during the first week, what he is going to have to do in the second; instead, he must work in the first week to obtain what he is looking for, just as if he did not hope to find anything good in the second week.

The one giving the Exercises ought carefully to warn the one receiving them that he must give an hour to each of the five exercises or contemplations which will be done each day; in this way, the retreatant will always have the satisfaction of thinking that he has been faithful in giving the whole hour to the exercise; and it is better for him to give more time rather than less. For it is a common temptation of the enemy to make us shorten the hour which we should be giving to contemplation, meditation or prayer.

All the same, we ought to note that, if it is easy, and not particularly burdensome, to stay at prayer for the whole hour in times of consolation, it is extremely difficult to finish the hour in times of desolation. This is why the one making the exercises must always persevere a little beyond the full hour, in order to fight against desolation and conquer temptations. By this means, he will accustom himself not only to holding firm against the adversary, but even to overwhelming him.

After this, Ignatius sketches out one of the first disciplines which he imposed on himself, and which he wishes to urge on his disciples: that self-control which each of them must use in order to govern their souls in the strictest manner possible.

So that the Creator and Lord might operate more surely within his creature, if it happens that this particular soul has a disordered affection or inclination for some object, it is extremely important for him to move his will, making every effort possible to bend it towards the contrary of the thing to which it is immoderately attached. For example, if he feels himself drawn to seek after and to possess an office or benefice, not for the motive of the honour and the glory of God our Lord, nor for the spiritual salvation of souls, but with his own advantage and his own temporal interests in view, he must direct his affections into the opposite channels, insisting on this point in his prayers and other spiritual exercises, and asking the Lord our God for the opposite thing to be given to him; finally, he will protest that he does not want the office or benefice, nor anything else in the world, unless the divine Majesty, restoring order to his desires, changes his first affection; in this way, the sole motive for desiring or possessing one thing or another, should be the service, honour and glory of the divine Majesty.

Not only prudence and discretion, but also vigilance, are demanded of the master whose task it is to support and to guide the first steps of the beginner.

Although the one giving the Exercises must not seek to know the private thoughts and sins of the one who is receiving them, nevertheless it is very useful that he should be faithfully informed of the various movements and thoughts which the various spirits stir up, because, depending on the fruit which the one receiving them is obtaining, it will be possible to make him do various spiritual exercises which would suit him and answer to the present needs of a soul troubled in that particular way.

So it seems clear that the *Exercises*, which were drawn up by a man who had only just escaped from the atmosphere of the military life, must be used in the way in which they were conceived—according to the same method and in the same spirit which guide an instructor given the task of forming a recruit. In a very strict and positive manner, he will make him do the exercises, training him and initiating him into the new form of life which awaits every civilian who becomes a soldier.

St Ignatius' *Spiritual Exercises* were soon used by him to fashion soldiers of God, who fought in his army and beat the enemy more easily for having first of all learnt to conquer themselves.

The first week: This is begun with a text which is so packed with matter, and which opens out on to such vast

horizons, that the impression is given that St Ignatius
wanted to condense a whole programme of action and life
for himself and for others into it. The title which he gave
to this exposition, which takes the form of an exordium, is
The Foundation; in it, he sets about defining the meaning
of human destiny, and the way it is to be worked out in
each of us.

> Man was created in order to praise, reverence and serve
> God our Lord and, by doing so, to save his soul. And the
> other things which we find on the face of the earth are
> created for man, in order to help him to reach the end for
> which he was created. From this it follows that man must
> use creatures to the extent that they help him to reach his
> end, and that he must abstain from them to the extent that
> they hinder him. This is why it is necessary for us to root
> ourselves in indifference towards all created things, in so far
> as this has been left to our free choice and is not forbidden,
> so that we should not, for our part, wish for health rather
> than sickness, for riches rather than poverty, for honour
> rather than contempt, for a long life rather than a short
> one, and so on for all the rest, desiring and choosing solely
> the things which will better lead us to the end for which we
> have been created.

Immediately after meditation nourished on this passage
with its wide horizons, we pass to two basic disciplines, on
which Ignatius builds up all his ascesis: the particular
examen and the general examen.

Here, his exposition suddenly takes on a practical, not to
say technical aspect: the particular examen should take
place on three occasions, while the general examen is
divided into five points.

The times for the particular examen:

> The first time is the morning: as soon as we get up, we
> form the resolution to guard vigilantly against the particular
> fault or sin of which we wish to correct and amend our-
> selves.

The second time is after dinner. First of all, we are to ask the Lord our God for what we desire—that is, the grace of remembering how many times we have fallen into this particular sin or fault, and that of amending for the future. Then we make the first examen, demanding an accurate account of our souls on the particular matter which we have proposed for ourselves, and of which we wish to correct and amend ourselves. To do this, we go over each hour, each space of successive time, from the moment when we got up to the time of the examen we are now making, and we mark a dot for each sin or fault we have committed. After this, we once again make a resolution to amend until the next examen.

The third time is after supper. We make the second examen in the same way, hour by hour, starting from the first, and we mark one dot for every time we have fallen into this particular sin or fault.

The points for the general examen:

The first is to thank the Lord our God for the benefits which we have received.

The second is to ask him to help us to know our sins and to expel them from our souls.

The third is to demand a faithful account of ourselves, from the time we got up to the time of this examen, going over all the hours or other successive periods of time to see whether we have failed, first of all in thought, then in word, and after this in deed, following the order laid down for the particular examen.

The fourth is to ask the Lord our God for pardon for our failures.

The fifth is to resolve to amend with the help of his grace.

Before all this, the retreatant will have studied with a great deal of care the attitude proper to this general examen, which is a direct preparation for confession, and which opens with this requirement: "I presume that there are three kinds of thought in me: one is my own, which

comes from my pure freedom and will; the two others
come from outside me, one through the promptings of the
evil spirit."

Ignatius thinks, and he is correct in doing so, that even
an evil thought is capable of acquiring merit for us, provided that we know how to reject it. It is in this way that
the brave battle which we wage against evil begins, to end
in victory.

> There are two ways of gaining merit when an evil thought
> comes to us from outside. For example, if the thought of
> committing a mortal sin comes to me, I can immediately
> resist it in such a way that it is overcome.
>
> The second way of meriting is when this same evil thought
> comes to me and I resist it; and then it returns twice or
> three times, and each time I go on resisting it, until this
> thought leaves in defeat; and this second way is of greater
> merit than the first.

The conditions for our defeat in this matter—and it is
equally important to know them, in order to be able to
eliminate them—are defined in an equally lucid manner:

> We sin venially when the thought of sinning mortally
> comes to us, and we listen to it, dwelling on it for a while,
> or receiving some sensual pleasure from it, or when there is
> some neglect on our part in rejecting the thought.
>
> There are two ways of sinning mortally. The first is when
> we consent to the thought, with the intention of acting after-
> wards in accordance with the consent we gave, or intending
> to put the thought into action if we could.
>
> The second way of sinning mortally is when we commit
> the sin by an exterior action, and this is more serious for
> three reasons: first of all because it lasts longer; secondly,
> because it reveals greater intensity on our part; and thirdly,
> because the harm done is greater for both persons.

We merit, and sin, just as much in word as in thought.
This is what Ignatius understands by useful and useless
speech:

We ought to avoid all idle words. By that, I mean words which are not useful either to myself or to others, and which are not intended to be useful. Thus, any time that some usefulness for my own soul, or for someone else's soul, or for the body, or for temporal good, either results from my words, or is intended to result from them, they will never be idle words, even though I may be talking about things which have nothing to do with my profession, as would happen, say, if a religious were to talk about war or business. But there is merit in everything that we say, provided that the speech is in order, and there is sin, if we speak with a disordered intention, or even without any reasonable motive.

Finally, we can sin in deed, in so far as we hold the ten commandments of God and the commandments of his Church in contempt.

We are to take the ten commandments of God, the commandments of the Church and the commands of our superiors as the subject matter for our examen. Anything which we do which is contrary to any of these three is a sin, which will be more or less serious according to the seriousness of the matter.

Here we can see how far the *Spiritual Exercises* push the science of introspection. A great fund of courage and lucidity is needed for it, as is universally agreed, as well as perfect humility of heart, together with an implacable severity towards oneself. But, once this preamble is over, we are ready to pass to the exercises proper of the first week. There are five of these, completed by ten additions, to which five observations are added. In his fearsome retreat at Manresa, Ignatius examined, imagined, foresaw, and resolved everything; he does not allow either himself or us the slightest indulgence; this sort of rigour is justified by what is at stake in the battle, namely, our eternal salvation and the greater glory of God.

Here there can be no question of exploring the whole

of the content of this first series of exercises. In this analysis of spiritual action elaborated by the new master of Christian asceticism, who was beyond the reach of compromise, the important thing was simply to reveal his system and to test its effectiveness; it would be impossible for anyone who adopted it to cheat his conscience and to compromise with sin. In this respect, Ignatius, after testing it on himself, provided each of us with a tool marvellously sharpened to penetrate into the most hidden corners of our souls and to purge them of every impurity.

What is more, the *Spiritual Exercises* form a whole, and make up a massive block, from which no single fragment can be isolated, for each is always conditioned by what has gone before, and is prolonged, without any loss of continuity, by the one which follows. To content oneself with reading any one particular text, even with the most scrupulous attention, would be to fly in the face of the plan which the author has maturely worked out; the work must be used like Ariadne's thread; it is designed to guide the conscience through the labyrinth of thought, word and deed which forms the life of every man, a dark road strewn with obstacles and pitted with insidious traps, on which temptation is widespread and virtue is constantly in peril for, at each step, a cunning spirit lies in ambush and tries to make us fall, as soon as we cease in the slightest degree to be on our guard as we arrive at this stage.

If we are to complete our survey of the main outlines of the Ignatian method, and to stress the originality, force and penetration which it brought into spiritual direction, it seems opportune at least to pause over some of the prominent points in the *Exercises*.

Thus, it is laid down, in the first exercise of this first week, that I must, by my preparatory prayer, "ask God our Lord for the grace always to direct my intentions, actions and works solely to the service and glory of his divine Majesty", and to talk to Jesus Christ "as a friend talks to his friend, or a servant to his master, now asking for a favour, now accusing myself of a fault, and now speaking about myself and asking advice"; in the second exercise, I am told to "ask for a great and intense sorrow for my sins, and for the tears with which to weep for them"; after thinking of the person of God, and considering against whom I have sinned, "I shall go over his divine attributes, comparing them with their opposites in me—comparing his wisdom with my ignorance, his infinite power with my weakness, his justice with my sin, and his goodness with my malice"; in the third exercise, I am to implore our Lady "to obtain for me from her Son and Lord, grace for this triple purpose: first, to have an intimate knowledge of my sins, and to detest them in the core of my soul; second, to feel the disorder of my actions in such a way, that, holding it in horror, I should reform and return to order; third, to know the world so well, that, in my aversion to it, I should drive all its vanities, and all that belongs to it, far from me"; in the fifth exercise, I am to beg, as its fruit, "intimately to feel the pain which the damned suffer, so that, if my faults ever should make me forget the love of the eternal Lord, at least the fear of punishment should help me to avoid falling into sin".

How, too, could we avoid lingering over the last of the ten additions (which all enrich this first cycle of exercises) which deals with penance? Because of its very rare quality, it deserves special attention, and it reveals the whole mind and character of the profound, subtle and penetrating Ignatius of Loyola:

> There are two sorts of penance: interior and exterior penance. Interior penance is sorrow for our sins, with a firm determination never again to commit either the same sins or others, no matter what they might be.
>
> Exterior penance, which is the fruit of this first sort,

consists in inflicting upon ourselves punishment for the sins which we have already committed. And this we do particularly in three ways:

The first is in matters of food. Here we ought to note that to deprive ourselves of what is superfluous is not penance but temperance. There is penance only in refusing ourselves what it is appropriate for us to have, and the more we go on refusing ourselves in this way, the greater and the better is the penance, provided that we do not go so far as to destroy our health or to contract a serious illness.

The second is in the way in which we take our sleep. Once again, it is not penance to refuse ourselves superfluous things which only encourage delicacy and softness. But there is penance in refusing ourselves, in this matter, what it is appropriate for us to have, and the more we succeed in cutting down in this way, the better is the penance, provided that it does not bring about a serious weakening of our strength or health. As far as sleep itself is concerned, we must not subtract anything from the proper amount, unless this is done in order to discover what is the right amount for us when we have to correct the vicious habit of oversleeping.

The third is to chasten our bodies, causing them sensible pain by using hairshirts, cords or iron chains which we wear close to the skin, by scourging ourselves, by inflicting wounds on ourselves, and by other rigours of this sort. What seems to be the most profitable and the least inconvenient plan is to cause the pain to be felt only in our skin, without penetrating to the bones, so that there will be pain, but no illness. This is why it seems better to use disciplines made of little cords, which cause exterior pain, rather than other means capable of producing any serious internal illness.

[And Loyola, who knew what he wanted and what he was doing, and why he wanted it and did it, ended with this:] External penances are practised for three principal reasons: firstly, as a satisfaction for past sins; secondly, in order to conquer ourselves, that is, so that sense appetites should obey reason, and so that the soul should keep greater control

over all its lower powers; thirdly, in order to obtain some
grace or favour which we may desire, such as to have an
intimate sorrow for our sins and a flow of tears with which
to weep for them, or to share in the pains and sufferings of
our Lord Jesus Christ in his Passion, or to receive the
solution to some doubt in which we find ourselves. . . .

When the one making the exercises still has not found
what he desires—such as tears or consolations—it is often
profitable to make some change in food, sleep and the other
exercises of mortification, so as to alternate, doing penance
for two or three days, and then omitting it for the next two
or three days; for it is important for some people to do
more penance, while others should do less. Often, too, we
omit the exercise of mortification through our sensuality,
and through the false idea that our health is going to suffer
serious harm; and sometimes, on the other hand, we do too
much, thinking that our bodies are going to be able to put
up with anything. But, since the Lord our God knows our
nature infinitely better than we do ourselves, he often makes
each of us feel, when we make this sort of change, what is
appropriate for us.

During the second week, a compact series of contemplations and meditations places the penitent in the presence
of the living Christ, and keeps him there, urging him to
unite himself to him in heart, mind and soul:

Those who wish to be more wholehearted, and who wish
to mark themselves out in everything to do with the service
of their eternal King and universal Lord, will not only
devote themselves completely to this work, but will also
take the offensive against their own sensuality and their
own fleshly and worldly love, by making gifts of greater
value and weight to him, saying: "O eternal Lord of all
things, relying on your favour and help, I make my obla-
tion before your infinite goodness, in the presence of your
glorious Mother and of all the saints of the heavenly court;
my will, my desire and my deliberate determination is to
imitate you by always bearing insults and contempt, as well

as every state of poverty, both actual and spiritual, provided that this is for your greater service and greater glory, if your most holy Majesty wishes to choose me and to accept me for this manner and state of life."

On the fourth day, we find the famous meditation on the two standards "the first, that of Jesus Christ, our supreme Leader and our Lord, and the second, that of Lucifer, the mortal enemy of human nature". Preludes and colloquies, in the fashion of a battle communiqué, bring the two adversaries to the scene, and then teach which of the parties, and which of the two standards we should choose, and how we are to fight against Lucifer, by the side of Jesus:

The first prelude, the historical view, will here show how Jesus Christ calls all men and desires them to be under his standard; and how Lucifer, on the other side, calls them and desires them to be under his standard.

The second prelude is the composition of place: here I shall imagine a vast plain taking in all that region of Jerusalem, where Jesus Christ is the supreme leader of the good; and another plain in the land of Babylon, where Lucifer is the leader of the enemy.

The third prelude is to ask for the fruit which I desire; here, I shall ask first for knowledge of the deceitfulness of the evil leader, and the help necessary to preserve myself from him, and secondly, the knowledge of the true life which the sovereign and true leader shows me, with the grace to imitate him.

First point: to imagine the leader of all the enemy in the middle of that vast plain of Babylon, seeing him seated in a great chair of fire and smoke, with a hideous and terrifying face.

Second point: to consider how he summons innumerable devils and sends them out, some to this town, and others to that, and so on throughout the world, omitting no single province, no single place, no single state, nor any single individual.

Third point: to consider the speech which he makes to them, and to consider how he commands them, with the use of threats, to set traps and chains. They are first to tempt men by the desire for riches (this is his practice with the majority of men) so as to succeed more easily in making them love the vain honour of the world, and then in urging them on to ever increasing pride. So that the first stage is riches, the second, worldly honour, and the third, pride; and from these three stages, Lucifer leads them on to all the other vices.

In the same way, on the opposite side, we must imagine the supreme and true Leader—our Lord Jesus Christ.

First point: to consider how our Lord Jesus Christ, comely and full of grace, occupies a humble place in the great plain of Jerusalem.

Second point: to consider how the Lord of the whole world chooses so many people—apostles, disciples and others—and sends them out into the wide world, to spread his sacred teaching among all states and conditions of men.

Third point: to consider the speech which our Lord Jesus Christ makes to all his servants and friends, whom he is sending out on this expedition. He urges them to desire to help all men, first of all by leading them to a complete poverty of spirit, and even, if the divine Majesty so pleases and if he desires to choose them, to actual poverty as well; secondly, by leading them to desire insults and contempt, because these two things bring humility in their train. In this way, there are three stages: the first is poverty, to combat riches; the second is insult or contempt, to combat worldly honour; and the third is humility, to combat pride; and from these three stages they will lead men on to all the other virtues.

Three colloquies—Ignatius was fond of using them—conclude this meditation on the two standards. He specifies that this important exercise must be made

at midnight, and, a second time, early in the morning; further, it must be repeated twice, once at the time of Mass, and once at the hour of Vespers, always ending with three colloquies to our Lady, to the Son, and to the Father:

Make a first colloquy to our Lady, asking her to obtain for me, from her Son and Lord, the grace of being received under his standard, first of all in complete spiritual poverty, and, if the divine Majesty so pleases and if he wishes to choose and receive me, even in actual poverty as well; after this, in the bearing of insult and derision, so as thus to imitate him more fully, provided that it will be possible for me to submit to this without anyone offending him, and without it causing displeasure to his divine Majesty.

Make a second colloquy to the Son to ask him to obtain the same grace for me from the Father.

Make a third colloquy to the Father, to ask him to deign himself to grant me this grace.

Once we have discovered the road which Ignatius trod and along which he leads us in the *Spiritual Exercises*, it seems almost impossible not to adopt it ourselves, and not to follow it, in his footsteps, right to the end.

The third and fourth weeks, during which the retreatant accompanies Christ in his passion, resurrection and ascension, leads him to the total possession of divine love, which has to be the sole aim, and the final term, of his earthly life. If we are docile to this masterly guide, we shall be encouraged to follow him, not only with our eyes and minds as we go through the text, but to give ourselves completely to his method, to put it into practice, and to make the *Exercises*, in an upsurge of our whole being, after choosing a director who is himself used to their disciplines and capable of helping us to draw from them all the fruit which they contain.

The other thing which this marvellous training of the soul achieves is to teach us, with complete lucidity, the primary duties of our state, that is, submission to the Church, the spouse of Christ, and the obligation to co-operate, by our works, in the action of grace and the play

of free will, and finally, without forgetting that love
ought always to be the real motive force behind everything
we do, always to live in the fear of God, which is the necessary complement to this love. This is the theme, upon
which it is very well worth meditating, of the last six
of the eighteen "rules of orthodoxy" with which the treatise
ends:

> In order to be sure of the truth in everything, it is
> necessary to adhere constantly to this principle, namely,
> that what I think to be white, I must believe to be black if
> the hierarchy of the Church defines it as such; persuading
> myself thoroughly that, between our Lord Jesus Christ, who
> is the Bridegroom, and the Church his Spouse, there is only
> one Spirit who governs us and rules us for the salvation of
> our souls, because this divine Spirit and Lord who gave us
> the ten commandments is the same who rules and governs
> our holy mother the Church.
>
> Although it is very true that no one can be saved if he is
> not predestined, and if he does not possess faith and grace,
> still, we must be very careful about how we speak about all
> these matters, and discourse on them.
>
> We must avoid saying very much, in an habitual manner,
> about predestination. But if we do say something about it,
> from time to time, we must do it in such a way that no
> occasion is given to the people to fall into any error and to
> say, as it often happens: "Whether I am to be saved or
> damned is something which has already been decided, and
> my good or evil works cannot change anything"; from this,
> drawing an occasion for relaxing, men would simply neglect
> the good works which help towards the salvation and the
> spiritual profit of their souls.
>
> For the same reason, when we talk at any length about
> faith, with the intention of exalting its excellence, but
> without making sufficient distinctions and without giving
> sufficient explanations, we must be careful not to give the
> people any opportunity to fall into carelessness and laziness
> on the subject of good works, either before charity has
> informed faith or afterwards.

In the same way again, we should not speak at great
length about grace, nor should we insist on it, in such a
way that our words produce the poison which destroys
liberty. This is why it is permissible for us to speak about
faith and grace, as far as we are able with the help of God,
for the greater glory of his divine Majesty, but we must not
do it, and particularly in times as dangerous as ours, by
using expressions which bring it about that good works and
free will suffer damage, or are counted for nothing.

While there is nothing more deserving of esteem than to
give ourselves completely to the service of the Lord our God
for motives of pure love for him, still we must greatly praise
the fear of his divine Majesty also, because not only is filial
fear a pious and very holy thing, but because servile fear
also, in cases when anyone cannot rise to anything better
and more profitable, gives him powerful help in leaving
mortal sin; and once he is saved from that, he can easily
arrive at that filial fear which is so pleasing and dear to the
Lord our God, since it is the inseparable companion to
divine love.

If Ignatius of Loyola had done nothing more than
compose the *Spiritual Exercises* and urge the men of his
age to practise them, he would still have done a great deal,
although not all that he was to do. After forging a wonderful instrument for spiritual conquest, it remained for him
to gather together, form and put to work those who would
be charged with putting it into action.

In this practical perspective, after Pamplona and Manresa, the third decisive stage of his life, divided as it was
between interior contemplation and the daily needs of
action, was Montmartre, where, on August 15th, 1534, with
six companions, who had all been won over by his teaching and asceticism, he took a vow, in all their names, on the
very spot where St Denis, the first bishop of Paris, was
thought to have been martyred, to live in poverty and
perfect chastity, and to leave for Jerusalem in order to
convert the infidels who were there.

These six pilgrims, all younger than himself, were students from the colleges of Montaigu and Sainte-Barbe, where he himself had come seven years earlier, after leaving Salamanca, to increase his general education which he thought to be too slight. Present on that spot were a Savoyard, Peter Faber, who had received the priesthood shortly before; a Navarrese, Francis Xavier; three Spaniards, Diego Laynez, Nicolas Bobadilla and Alonso Salmeron; and a Portuguese, Simon Rodriguez. When they took their solemn vow, Ignatius of Loyola made the supplementary vow to take the road to Rome, if their expedition to Palestine should prove impossible, and there place himself under the direct orders of the pope. And this was what they did in the end. On this beautiful day of the Assumption, an apostolic army, destined to become famous, was born—an incomparable instrument of conquest in the hands of the Catholic Church, and an inexhaustible reservoir of men of action, knowledge and high virtue—the Society of Jesus.

When, on September 27th, 1540, the pope, Paul III, published his Bull *Regimini militantis Ecclesiae*, giving canonical status to the Society, he accomplished one of the most important acts for which the papacy has been responsible. For the members of the Society immediately signed the written vow which committed them to go immediately wherever the pope should think it useful to send them, to pagans and infidels, to schismatics and heretics, as well as among the faithful, to instruct them all in the true faith. And each committed himself, in addition, to obey his superior, Ignatius of Loyola, *perinde ac cadaver*, as passively as a corpse.

Formed in the school of the *Spiritual Exercises*, and governed by the *Constitutions* with which their leader provided them, this exemplary army, sprung from the will, holiness and genius of the man whom God had drawn from the gutter in order to raise him to the most glorious of earthly destinies, was going to become, and to remain, the militant wing of the Catholic army, the iron lance of the papacy, wielding the sword of faith and bearing the standard of Christ in the struggle in which it was to face, and overwhelm, the infernal legions under obedience to Lucifer.

In this way, for the greater glory of God, the Church acted through St Ignatius.

CHAPTER VI

THE SAINTS THROUGH WHOM THE CHURCH ACTS

If it is undoubtedly true that these men—the Jew, the African, the Burgundian, the Umbrian and the Basque—were among the greatest of the saints chosen by God to enable his Church to act through them, they must not make us forget that there were a host of others, whom he chose, and whom she adopted, who played their part, at the right hour, in the right place, and in the right circumstances, in the concerted action which Rome, Christ's earthly capital, brought to bear on the pagan world, on those who had separated from the true faith, and on the Catholic community itself, a prey to the uncertainties, the weaknesses and the desertions which are the lot of all human societies. This is what happened from the very earliest days of the Church, and this is what happened at each dangerous turning-point in her history; this, too, is what is happening today, and this is what will go on happening until the end of time, when, at the Parousia, Jesus Christ, the Son of God, will return to this earth to judge mankind which will then have reached the final term of its destiny.

In apostolic times, when the only need, after the Master

had gone, was to bear witness, to Jews and Greeks, of his divine mission, the Twelve acquitted themselves by the spoken and written word and, with the exception of John, by the bloody sacrifice of their lives, of the task which Jesus had laid upon them, that is, to carry his holy message to the ends of the known world. After James the Less, the leader of the community in Jerusalem, had been the first to be martyred, Peter and the others, in their turn, poured out the tribute of their blood and, all through the second century, they were followed along that purple road by which Christianity was advancing through the pagan world, by hundreds of their brethren: Ignatius at Antioch, Polycarp at Smyrna, and Pothinus at Lyons, as well as the two heroic brides of Christ, Blandina at Lyons again, and Caecilia in Rome.

At that time, it was enough to proclaim oneself a Christian to be consigned immediately to the gallows, the sword or the jaws of the wild animals. In the same way, during the following two centuries, under the emperors Septimius Severus, Decius, Valerian and Diocletian, those witnesses of Christ whose names still shine in the martyrology died a horrible death with thousands of others, at the hands of the executioners—Perpetua, a noble woman,˙ Cyprian, the bishop of Carthage, Pope Fabian, Denis, the bishop of Paris, Saturninus of Toulouse, Polyeuctes, an Armenian lord, Pionius, a priest of Smyrna, Pope Sixtus II, the child Cyril in Cappadocia; Sebastian, a tribune, Agnes, a Roman virgin, Pope Marcellinus, Lucy of Syracuse, Pamphylius, a Palestinian priest, Felix, the bishop of Africa, Irene of Salonica, Hermes, deacon of Heracleus, Cosmas and Damian, both doctors from Arabia, Margaret of Antioch, and Catherine of Alexandria, and finally Maurice, a tribune belonging to the Theban legion.

By signing the Edict of Milan in 313, Constantine, who had defeated his rival Maxentius at the Milvian Bridge, stemmed this stream of blood. In the words of Daniel-Rops, the Revolution of the Cross had succeeded. The Church, acting through her martyrs, had triumphed over Roman paganism.

At the same time, she struck deadly blows at pagan thought, through the inspired pens of her first doctors, the apologists. Following in the footsteps of Matthew, Mark and Luke, authors of the synoptic Gospels and of the Acts of the Apostles, John, the beloved disciple, by writing the Apocalypse, during his exile at Patmos, created the earliest monument of Christian literature, and had followed this at Ephesus by writing his Gospel, the source for all theology.

After John's death, Justin, who had been formed in the school of Aristotle and Plato, emigrated from Caesarea in Palestine to Ephesus, and then to Rome, at the beginning of the second century, and, with his "Dialogue with Trypho" and his "Apologies", opened the age of a new philosophy, which sprang directly from the thought of Christ the teacher, but which used the vocabulary and preserved the methods of thought held in repute among the thinkers of ancient Greece. When he was called upon to retract by Rusticus, a prefect under Marcus Aurelius, he chose to die by the sword rather than stop writing.

Forty years later, the torch which had fallen from his hands was picked up by Irenaeus, bishop of Lyons. This Greek from Smyrna had drunk at the fount of apostolic tradition and of the purest Christology: Polycarp had handed on to him what he himself had received from John, and what John, in turn, had received from Jesus. Irenaeus, himself formed in the Greek disciplines, and a Roman by adoption, chose to become a Westerner among the Gauls of Lyons, and, to protect his flock from the heresy which was then being spread by the Gnostics, used the heretics' own vocabulary and closely followed the line of their thought. Irenaeus held that reason had to be directed by faith, while Justin, at the opposite pole of Christian dialectics, had maintained, equally justly, that reason was included in faith. But both were to establish a vital point in the action which the Church carried out through her writers: the only guiding points for faith are to be found in Tradition, a spiritual highway which begins in the Old Testament, passes through the New, and leads, apart from the deviations of any personal interpretation or personal system, to the kingdom of God, which is the final term for all men, who have been instructed by Jesus' teaching and redeemed by his sacrifice on Calvary.

The same spiritual combat was to be waged in the fourth century, under the aegis of the Church and in her service, by three valiant champions of Christian thought—Athanasius, the bishop of Alexandria and Hilary, the bishop of Poitiers, who both inflicted crushing defeats on Arianism, and Ambrose, the noble archbishop of Milan, who brought about within himself, in a wonderful harmony, an intimate and fruitful fusion of realistic action, creative thought and life in God.

Throughout this extraordinary century, which was closed in 380 by the decree of the Emperor Theodosius which declared that the whole population of the empire had to adhere to the Christian faith, the Church once more acted through the individual geniuses (all directed to very different ends) of Jerome, John Chrysostom, Antony, Pachomius and Basil in the East, and of Martin in the West, all of them great saints.

Jerome, a native of Croatia, left Rome for Bethlehem, where, in solitary retreat, he built up the literary production, of unusual dimensions, which showed him to be, in turn, a philosopher, a scholar, a rhetorician, a grammarian and a dialectician—a man capable of writing and thinking in Hebrew, Greek and Latin, and of using a vocabulary which was rich, pure and full of savour. His most important work was his Latin translation of the Old and the New Testaments which, under the name of the Vulgate, became the official Bible of the West. His contemporary, John Chrysostom, who was born and baptized at Antioch, returned to that city after spending six years in the desert, and immediately began a preaching career, in which he shone with outstanding brilliance. The hundreds of his sermons and homilies which have been preserved reveal an oratorical genius making "St John of the Golden Mouth" the earliest, and probably the greatest, of the sacred orators through whose eloquence the Church acted on the multitudes.

However, another great current of Christian spirituality, the source of an institution which was to have as much and, in some ways, even greater importance in the activity of the Church than the foundation of missionary teams or the proliferation of priestly communities and intellectual schools, originated in the East and took root there, through the genius of three giants of sanctity, Antony and Pachomius, Christians from Egypt, and Basil, the light of Cappadocia: the first began the eremitical life, made up of solitude and mortification; the second instituted the cenobitical life, based on communal life in penance and prayer; the third provided cenobitical life with its organic laws by producing the earliest monastic rule enjoining strict enclosure, collective prayer, obligatory manual work and intellectual culture directed towards study of, and meditation on, the sacred texts.

From the East, monasticism very quickly spread to the West, where Martin of Poitiers planted it first at Ligugé, and then at Marmoutier, near Tours, where he had become bishop. With Martin, the apostle of the Gauls, the monks of the West, unlike their brothers in the East, who were exclusively dedicated to the life of contemplation, asserted their second vocation: they soon became missionaries, and thanks to their spirit of conquest, pagan Europe, from Ireland to Germany, and from Poland to Spain, joined the Church of Christ, amid the din of broken idols and destroyed temples.

From this conquering epic, there emerged the pioneers who, all through the barbarian period, were to plant the cross on all the horizons of the Western world.

One of the first of these was Severinus, a Roman knight. In the middle of the fifth century, he came to the Danube to build a monastery which, because of his extreme charity, became a centre of attraction for the German peoples, who until then had supported Arianism in a body. By doing this, he paved the way for the man who was to become the great apostle of Germany some two and a half centuries later, Boniface, an English monk. Originally, he was called Winfrid, and he had been born in Wessex and had taught at the monastery of Nursling; Pope Gregory II made him his personal envoy in Germany, and he conquered it acre by acre, and soul by soul, for Christ and, as archbishop of Mainz, placed it, from Bavaria to the Zuider Zee, under the rule of the Roman pontiff.

At the end of the sixth century, his own country had been evangelized, on the instructions of Pope Gregory the Great, by Augustine, the prior of the Roman monastery on the Coelian Hill. At that time, Britain was held under the yoke of her Anglo-Saxon conquerors, and the primitive Celtic Church had with difficulty just escaped destruction. Augustine, carrying high the emblem of Christ, won over King Ethelbert, who was baptized by him, with all his court, at Pentecost in the year 597. The following Christmas, the apostle, who multiplied miracles wherever he went, baptized ten thousand islanders in one day, and, after being promoted archbishop of Canterbury, founded the Church in England.

Christian Ireland had also survived the occupation and awaited spiritual liberation from the end of the third century. It was brought to them in the first half of the fifth century by one of their own people, Patrick, a monk of the Mediterranean island of Lérins, who had become a missionary with the blessing of Germanus of Auxerre; Patrick, as fertile in miracles as Augustine, succeeded in drawing the country away from the domination of the Druids, and when he died, it was already being called the Island of Saints.

This same Ireland, where Catholicism had thus taken root, never to disappear, gave birth in 540 to the most outstanding pioneer on pagan soil produced by an age rich in apostles; this was Columba, a monk of Bangor, in Ulster. He was a healer and a prophet, a man of God, a force of nature, and a genius who, for forty years, sowed the seed of Christ by the armful in the furrows which he had ploughed from Rouen to Coblenz, and from Nantes to Milan, and who harvested souls by the thousand.

Finally, the regions to the north and east, on the borders of the Continent (where the future shape of Europe was already beginning to be seen) had to wait until the ninth century before seeing the cross set up and flourishing under their hostile skies. At that time, the Church, which had suffered the murderous assault of the Normans, made a counter-attack, and sent Anskar to the land of the Vikings. Setting out alone from his Saxon abbey of Corbie, Anskar, who was a monk, set up his missionary base in Hamburg; from there, he radiated out into Denmark and Sweden, standing firm when the devastating raids of the men of Norway broke over his young Christian communities; in this way, with quiet heroism, he established valuable outposts all along the road which was later to lead to a Christian Scandinavia.

Twenty years after him, two brothers, who were Greeks

from Thessalonica, approached the world of the Slavs, then sunk in its barbaric fogs, from the East. Their names were Cyril and Methodius. Moravia was their first conquest, a conquest which their successors succeeded in extending to Bulgaria. Next came the turn of the Serbs. Nor did the Russians have long to wait: as the year 1000 was drawing close, Vladimir, still a half-pagan savage, and the grandson of Prince Igor and of Olga, a Christian princess, undertook to convert them in his own characteristic way, after the manner of the Cossacks. This was his way to God, and later it led him to penance and sanctity. In fact, Byzantium had been more active in this region than Rome. But this was not true in Hungary; Pope Sylvester II anointed Stephen as its apostolic king; he turned this land, settled by the Magyars, into the most Catholic kingdom of Europe. Stephen was canonized.

By leaving their cloisters in such numbers to go out to the four corners of the West and plant new Christian communities, the apostolic monks sacrificed contemplation to action, to the detriment of their original vocation. It is true that the Church encouraged them in this, and nearly all the popes, up to the year 1000, justified this activity (for which the Church mobilized the best, greatest and holiest of them) by the need to break the soil of pagan Europe. Apart from this consideration, we have also to take into account the fact that the monastic life in the West had not yet found its legislators, as it had done in the East, and was still in an imperfect, and even occasionally anarchical, state. Martin at Ligugé and at Marmoutier, Cassian at Marseilles, and, above all, Honoratus at Lérins, by their personal influence and the radiation of their interior life, had each managed to group together communities in which contemplative vocations could flourish. But these were only local experiments, and they were not to survive their founders, nor were they to spread beyond their point of origin.

It fell to Benedict of Nursia to provide Western monasticism with its statutes and with its possibilities of expansion. This he did at Monte Cassino, after testing his ascetical system in the grotto at Subiaco, by writing and applying his Rule, a masterpiece of psychology, and a lofty monument of spirituality which established the unity of the cenobitical society, developed in the East by Pachomius and Basil, on firm foundations. Between the death of the patriarch, in 547, and the end of the eleventh century, when it was to be reformed, the Benedictine order expanded in an extraordinary way, placing its innumerable abbeys and priories, which were filled with saints, at the service of the Church, for her work of civilization and for her plans for spiritual conquest.

The hierarchical Church itself, in the person of popes and bishops, produced giants of sanctity, whose activity, at its peak, served both as a driving force and as an example.

The two most outstanding Roman pontiffs of that age were Leo I, the Great, who reigned from 440 to 461, and the Roman patrician who had become a monk, and who ascended the throne of Peter in 590 under the name of Gregory the Great. The first drove back Attila and his yellow knights, when the general Aetius had proved incapable of blocking their way to Rome, and thus helped to turn the ancient city of the Caesars into the capital of the Christian world; from that moment, the popes were to reign in Rome in all the splendour of their spiritual primacy. The second, ruling in a Rome which was a prey to schism, famine and plague, courageously faced the perils which were attacking the Church, and by his universal genius, which, as he himself said, was nourished on the "pure wheat" of St Augustine, made the papacy shine with the brightness of its universal power, and, by the new vitality which he communicated to the missions, made it possible for the West, submerged beneath the barbarian tide, to be reconquered.

Around these two exceptional pontiffs, who were to add the halo of sanctity to the brightness of their tiaras, it was no longer possible to count the bishops of that time destined to the glory of the altars by their heroism, their genius or their piety. The earlier group had faced the pagan invasion with Leo, and had defended their cities against it: of these, Nicasius, Aignan, Lupus, Sidonius Apollinarius and Germanus of Auxerre seem to have been the most glorious. Their successors, with equal energy and a similar aptitude for sanctity, undertook the task of turning the idolatrous Germans, the masters of the lands of the West, into Christians. Some of these bishops were diplomats of great ability, and here politics were merged with the apostolate. They had seen that it was enough for them to convert the leaders for the mass of the warriors to agree, in turn, to being baptized. Remigius, the bishop of Rheims, excelled in this subtle strategy, and the prey which he brought in homage to Christ was a great one in Clovis, King of the Franks.

In his task, he was helped by Clotilda, the wife of the conqueror of Tolbiac, the daughter of Childeric, and a Christian; so true is it that, in order to win a man, the help of his wife is necessary above all else. From that moment, the Church was to act frequently through women, provided that the women were saints. There was one shepherdess who turned the hordes of Attila from Paris merely by praying; her name was Geneviève, and, in her old age, she became a friend of Queen Clotilda, who had brought about the christianization of the Franks.

In fact, through these terrible years when the very existence of the Church was at stake, the Church of Jesus Christ survived and became what she still is today through the action of those of her monks, kings, popes, bishops, princesses and shepherdesses who bore on their foreheads the golden halo of sanctity.

The following age was the age of triumph; and it was also the time when sanctity flowered in exuberant blooms within the garden of the Church. This period has been called the Middle Ages, but this is a misnomer: it was not a period of transition; it does not form a shadowy passageway from the barbarian night to a Renaissance flooded with pagan light; it was not a pathway, but a summit, reaching up into the open sky, on which the society of Christ built up its divine structures, by the hands of men who were guided and supported by their faith in Christ as God and King; it was the age of Christendom; the centuries of the true light which enlightens every man who comes into this world—the light to which the men of that world did not shut their eyes and the light which radiated from the genius of Bernard of Fontaines, Francis of Assisi, Dominic of Caleruega, Albert the Great, Bonaventure, Thomas Aquinas, Pope Gregory VII and Louis IX, king of France—through all of whom the Church acted even more vigorously than before in this golden age of the faith.

The saints of the centuries of victory arose in such tremendous numbers that we cannot attempt to portray even the greatest of them in our historical window—a window so vast that it could not be fitted into a cathedral higher than the cathedral of Beauvais, and as wide as Beauvais was intended to be in the dreams of its mad master of works—vast as such a cathedral would be. Among them were monks and apostles: Bruno of Cologne, a student at Paris, and a teacher of theology at Rheims, came to the desert of Chartreuse, and there, in 1084, founded the first monastery to bear its name, the monastery which was to be the head of an Order made up of a religious élite whose vocation it was to occupy the highest peak in the contemplative hierarchy; Robert of Molesmes, a Benedictine belonging to the congregation of Cluny, founded, in March 1098, with Alberic and Stephen Harding, the "New Monastery", hidden in the harsh woods of Cîteaux, where they restored the Rule of St Benedict to its original purity; Norbert of Xanten, sprung from noble Rhineland stock, a favourite of his cousin, Emperor Henry V, a canon possessed of ample wealth and little virtue, took off his fur-lined coat and his silk soutane one fine day, and put on the rags of a wanderer of Christ (just as Francis and Ignatius were to do after him) and preached repentance and judged disputes, before establishing the Order of Prémontré in the frozen heart of the forest of Coucy, on Christmas night, 1121—an Order which was soon rich in monk-priests who preserved the legacy of this apostolic soul, with his eagerness for conquest, and made it bear fruit; Dominic of Caleruega, another canon regular, but from Castille this time and not from Germany, who had a burning soul and an imperious heart, and whose voice resounded like bronze, was discouraged by Pope Innocent III from going to evangelize the Kumans of Hungary, and was commissioned, on the pope's command, for the even more difficult task of crossing swords with the Cathari of Languedoc, violent heretics; Dominic left his chapter in Osma in order to put on the black and white serge, take to the road and go and lavish the charity of the truth on those who had gone astray, at every crossroad from Toulouse to Carcassonne, bringing them back to the fold more surely than Simon of Montfort with his knights was to do; then, at Prouille, at the foot of the Pyrenees, he set up the first stage of the holy journey which was going to lead his sons to the ends of the world, after Honorius III had instituted, in the winter of 1216, the Friars Preachers—the second in date of the Mendicant Orders and the one which was to be, as the clear-sighted pope proclaimed, "the champion of the faith, and the true light of the world".

Then there were bishops and doctors: Anselm served the Church illustriously in both capacities, opposing the rampart of his inflexible will against abuses of the temporal power, when he occupied the archiepiscopal see of Canterbury, and forced the English King, Henry I Beauclerc, to capitulate; at the same time, he opened the way for scholasticism by his writings, and justified his dialectic by referring to a principle which was to become famous: "I do not seek to understand in order to believe; I believe in order to understand"; in face of Henry II Plantagenet, Thomas Becket, another archbishop of Canterbury, raised the iron shield of the Church against the encroachments of the brutal monarch; when he returned to his cathedral, from Sens where he had been forced to take refuge, he was thrown down from his throne and died, on December 29th, 1170, beneath the swords of the king's supporters. A hundred years later, three of the greatest intellects to shine in this age of light, were to raise aloft the sword of the same triumphant Church—a sword with Christian thought sparkling on its point; one of them was a son of St Francis, and the other two were sons of St Dominic; they were the champions of pure speculation, and the heroes of scholasticism, and they all depended (particularly the latter two), on the disciplines of Aristotle, who had been neglected by their predecessors, since St Augustine, in favour of Plato; their names were John of Fidanza, called Bonaventure by Francis of Assisi, a mystic and a philosopher; Albert the Great, the universal Doctor; and Thomas Aquinas, the angelic Doctor, whose superhuman genius is radiated by his *Summa Theologica*.

Then there were kings and popes; one of the most outstanding popes ever to rule the Church was Hildebrand, first a Benedictine monk of Saint Mary on the Aventine and then a cardinal, who was finally raised to the throne of St Peter by popular acclaim; he received the tiara, in the summer of 1073, after being ordained, and became Gregory VII; his character was as strong as steel, he was lucid and filled with energy, unaffected by diversity, and possessed the Roman sense of the Church and of the dignity of his supreme pastorate; but he was a humble man, despite the danger of a towering mind; his soul was imbued with spirituality, and open to the infinite horizons of the supernatural; he was a saint who could also be a profound, subtle and shrewd politician, who restored moral integrity to the Catholic clergy, and independence from lay power to the Church, negotiating in a decisive manner with kings, without ever withdrawing a step and without making a mistake.

Gregory was a giant in the papacy; of less stature, admittedly, but filled with the key qualities which produce exceptional pontiffs, Innocent III, who became pope at the age of thirty-eight, did at least two things in his eighteen-year reign which would assure him of imperishable fame; he provided the Church with new apostles, when he realized the capabilities of Francis and Dominic, and, a hundred years after Gregory VII, he gave proof of a political genius equal to that of his predecessor and affirmed the supremacy of the bishop of Rome over all the thrones of the earth when he threatened Philip Augustus with his apostolic power after reminding him that "the royal dignity cannot transcend the duties of a Christian"; of the crowned heads of that time, two at least, both destined to sanctity, bowed the prestige attached to their diadems before the majesty of the Vicar of Jesus Christ: Ferdinand III, the Holy, the Spanish monarch, "a knight of Christ, a servant of God, and the standard bearer of my Lord St James", who drove the Moors from Cordoba after inflicting on them their first bloody defeats, and, secondly, and above all, Louis IX, king of France by divine grace, the son of Blanche of Castile, a simple pilgrim on earth marching to the heavenly kingdom, and a tertiary of the order of St Francis; he was a true monarch, skilled in government, a knight in the service of the Lord God, a mine of charity, a well of mercy; he was the father of eleven children and the chastest of men; he was the very embodiment of Christendom—that glorious daughter of the Church, which, from the eleventh century to the fourteenth, established the reign of Christ over the kingdoms of this earth.

And, finally, there were the women saints of the Middle Ages, the blossoms of those four centuries of which the humiliated Christians of our own age cannot help dreaming: Hildegarde, Gertrude, Elizabeth of Schönau, Mechtild of Hackeborn, Angela of Foligno and Catherine of Siena who were all mystics who had escaped from the earth, visionaries and prophetesses whose message was received in trembling by the leaders of the Church; Bridget of Sweden, who also spoke out loud and clear, and the poignant Elizabeth of Hungary, who immolated her life to care for lepers —all these, and all the others, showed at that time, by their sublime or heroic virtues, that women were capable of equalling, if not surpassing, men in sanctity; but this was something which was already known, by the grace given to her to whom the Middle Ages, through the mouth of Bernard of Clairvaux, paid the homage of its love, and whom it named as its Lady—Mary, the holiest of God's creatures, whom God chose for his Mother, and whom he gave to us all as our own mother on Golgotha.

The last quarter of the fourteenth century, however, was to see new dangers spring up and grow larger on the horizon—dangers which were soon to fall upon the Church.

Gregory XI, the latest of the Avignon popes, brought the Holy See back to Rome. He died there some months later, in 1378. The Roman cardinals elected Urban VI; but Avignon also chose a Pontiff in Clement VII. The Great Schism of the West had begun. Now the Church of Christ had two heads, just as in the time of Anacletus. She was even to finish by having three, when Pisa conferred the tiara on Alexander V. Finally, in 1417, the Council of Constance brought this anarchy to an end.

Christendom was not to survive this, since it was built up on the monolithic unity of the Roman Church. And this unity seemed to be completely compromised, from outside as well as from within. The Hundred Years War was ravaging the West. Authority, moral strictness, intellectual vigour and spiritual vitality had deserted the ranks of the Catholic clergy. As the fifteenth century went by, the splits grew wider, and cracks reaching down to the foundations of the Church shook the Christian edifice. In 1453, the Turks were at Constantinople. John Huss, a priest from Prague, and the heir to the Vaudois, had been executed, but he was to pave the way for heresy. Neither Luther nor Calvin were yet born; but henceforward, Luther and Calvin would both be possible; and they would be even more possible after Rome decided to provide itself with popes who were simoniacs, politicians, warriors, humanists or worse, with Sixtus IV, Innocent VIII, Alexander VI, Julius II and Leo X: Rome, now raised to the dignity of the capital of the arts, had ceased to be the metropolis of the faith.

At this moment, almost as if she herself secreted an antidote for the pernicious evil which was gnawing at her, the Church raised up saints whose virtue and genius were to grow as the dangers became more precise.

First of all there were two women, whose origins were as diverse as their destinies, two virgins who, even so, were cousins, with such a stoutness of soul, and such a purity of heart that the men of their time knelt before them: they were Colette of Corbie, the recluse who set off on the roads of the West to bring vigour and integrity back to the monasteries of St Clare, and who one day brought the anti-pope Benedict XIII to her feet solely by the light which illumined her face; and Joan of Domrémy, Joan of Arc, "our Joan", as the French call her, whose knees were embraced by La Hire and Dunois, the Maid, a proud instrument of God, whom she served first of all, in restoring peace to the land of France, a shepherdess who outwitted theologians, whose body was to be consumed by the flames at Rouen, but whose heart they were powerless to reduce to ashes—Joan who was great because she suffered, not for the Church, but at the hands of the Church, and whom the Church was to take from the fire of infamy and set on the sacred pedestal of her altars.

Like these two daughters of God, Bernardino of Siena, John of Capistran, Antoninus of Florence and Francis of Paula were also to put up a good fight. But Luther and Calvin had already waged their own battle, and had won it; and so had Henry VIII of England. It seemed that the Church would never again regain her strength and her greatness. But, more surely than the Council of Trent, which opened in December 1545, two months before Luther died, a woman was once more helping in making the Church strong and in building it up on a worldwide scale. And of this woman it has been said that she was a wonderful man of action.

She was Teresa de Cepeda. This noble daughter of Avila, who loved to laugh, sing and dance all her life and who was pierced by Jesus with his sword of love, all through her earthly life alternated between heavenly ecstasy and the most worldly tasks, but without losing her balance for a moment as a consequence. In her heart, there dwelt the flame which produces heroes; her mind shone with lucid intelligence; and in her soul, she attained to the total possession of God. With these weapons, she carried out a task which today seems to us to be a superhuman one. From the convent of St Joseph, outside the walls of her own city of Avila—the first Carmelite convent which she had reformed—she set out, loaded with the treasures of her "interior castle", on the rough roads of Spain, where her opponents, the "mitigated" Carmelites, were lying in wait for her. But she was to meet someone who would help her conquer them—her brother in Christ, John of the Cross, a Carmelite sprung from the race of the hidalgos, who had been quick to make his escape from Salamanca, haunted like her by the thought of the ancient greatness of the Order, to which, united in spirit and action with Teresa, he was to restore its integrity. In the monasteries which the two of them peopled with Carmelite friars and nuns in their white cloaks, there still resounds today the echo of his *Spiritual Canticle*, a hymn of souls visited by heaven, which was to be sung in the same inspired tones, some three centuries later in the Carmel of Lisieux, by the child who was also called Teresa, and who proved that the Church will always have saints to act in her name.

Among those who still fought for the Church while heresy was tearing at her, and while renewed paganism was threatening to drown her, a large place must be given to Charles Borromeo: he had hardly seemed to be on the road to sanctity when he was made a cardinal, at the age of twenty-two, by his uncle Pius IV, who nominated him, in record time, Secretary of State, archbishop of Milan, protector of Portugal and of Lower Germany, legate of Bologna, protector of the Carmelites, of the Canons of Coimbra, of the Franciscans, and of the Order of Christ, archpriest of St Mary Major, and Grand Penitentiary, with something like 50,000 crowns a year in benefices; he was a wealthy prince of the Church, and yet, showered with so much honour, power and wealth, he lived the life of an ascetic, in the school of Ignatius, working like an ox, refusing the tiara (preferring instead to turn his archdiocese of Milan, then largely undeveloped, into an exemplary region of the Church), giving himself prodigally, beyond the bounds of charity and the records of heroism, during the devastating plague of 1576, and dying, at the age of forty-six, just as he had lived, like a saint. We must allot an equal place to Philip Neri: he had been born in Florence among the people, and he was to belong to the people all through a life crammed with audacity, tricks and pranks which endeared him to the people of Rome, whom he gathered together in the streets, and who, won over by him, followed him to the confessional; he was a great mystic and was favoured with conversations with the Master; he was a visionary and a prolific worker of miracles; he also founded the Oratory, without really planning it, where he introduced new disciplines which were always within the capacities of the people, and which were motivated solely by love; this was Philip Neri, God's fool, who proclaimed, and preached by his example, that all we have to do here on earth is to live in God and to die to self. Finally, we must give an equally important place to Robert Bellarmine: from his youth, he was one of Loyola's most effective disciples, and neither Luther nor Calvin were to have a more redoubtable opponent than the author of the *Controversies*—a massive treatise in which their doctrines are objectively presented, and refuted point by point, with a vigour and a lucidity of thought which betrayed genius.

In Bellarmine, the Church was to have not only one of the last of her Doctors, but the principal promoter of an instrument which was responsible for the fact that the Catholic faith was borne far across the seas to all the peoples of the earth: this was the Roman Congregation for the Propagation of the Faith, to which the Church's missionary activity owed its prodigious expansion. For now that the Church was being threatened, she did not content herself with facing the heresy, but soon passed from the defensive to the offensive, and, from the lands of the Christendom, where she refused to yield an inch, carried her fight to those countries where the pagan peoples had not yet received the message of Christ. Here a great pioneer had traced out the road on which Dominicans, Franciscans, Capuchins and Jesuits were to follow in his footsteps: this was Francis of Jassu, Lord of Xavier, one of Ignatius' first companions, and a Basque like him, who had been formed in his ascetical method; he was a mystic involved in action, as Daniel-Rops has rightly pointed out, just like Bernard of Clairvaux, Joan of Arc, Louis IX and Teresa of Avila, for all of whom action was only "the visible expression, one might say the projection, of their inner experience"; Francis Xavier, the conqueror of the Indies, where the primitive Christianity which Thomas Didymus had planted in apostolic times, welcomed the flame of Christ; Francis Xavier, the first to cultivate the soil of Malaysia, the Islands of Sonde, the Moluccas and Japan, who gave back his great soul to God in sight of the coasts of China, where the Cross, thanks to him, was to be set up by other hands.

Nineteen years after his death, Asia, to which he had carried the Gospel of Jesus Christ with open arms and open heart, the unbelieving Asia of the Turks, suffered its final defeat on October 7th, 1571, in the gulf of Lepanto, at the hands of Don John of Austria: the cross was triumphing over the crescent, at the end of a battle soon to reach its thousandth year, and the artisan of this lofty victory was St Pius V, the last of the pontiffs, before St Pius X, whom the Church has raised to her altars, the Dominican Michael Ghislieri. He was Caraffa's assistant at the head of the Holy Office, and then himself became Inquisitor General; he was an ascetic pope who had a cell arranged for him in the Vatican, where he lived on bread and water, and who one day gave the Church over which he ruled a lesson, which it is good for her to ponder on, to guide her action, as he addressed his cardinals: "It is to us, the light of the world and the salt of the earth, to whom belongs the task of enlightening spirits and of animating hearts by the example of our sanctity."

The two saints who led the Church, worn out by now by her double fight against the Renaissance and the Reformation, into the modern era, were of such great stature and of such wide intellect, that it would be very natural for us to assume that they were announcing and inaugurating a new age of sanctity, one brighter than all the others. But, as it became clear, they were not, in fact, the advance guard of an army capable of meeting, and defeating, an enemy which was to make the enemies of the past seem, by comparison, not ridiculous, but isolated aggressors; it was after them that men arose, grimly determined to banish God from the hearts of their fellows, to kill him in their souls, and to banish him from a society which found its ideal in life and the final fulfilment of its destiny in opposition to him. Francis de Sales and Vincent de Paul were only snipers, just as Francis Regis, John Eudes, Grignion de Montfort, John Baptist de la Salle, Isaac Jogues, Jean de Brébeuf, Benedict Labre, Alphonsus de Liguori, Jean-Marie Vianney and John Bosco were, in face of the Jansenism of Port-Royal, the absolutism of the "most Christian" king, the Gallicanism of a domesticated clergy, the paganism of still barbarian peoples, the atheism of Diderot, the Jacobinism of Robespierre, the police state of Napoleon, the liberalism of Lammennais, the nationalism of Bismarck, the materialism of Karl Marx, and the Masonic intrigues of Cavour and Garibaldi.

The question which we have now to ask is whether the stream of sanctity was suddenly threatening to dry up, or whether the action of the saints during the seventeenth, eighteenth and nineteenth centuries was no longer, as it used to be, the ideal instrument of defence and conquest which the Church had used to ward off all attacks and to carry her power to the ends of the earth. In fact, there seems no doubt to the impartial historian that, although the papacy still continued, as the guardian of the faith, to fulfil the task entrusted by Christ to Peter and his successors, it also presented the sad sight of failure when faced by a world shaken by frightening upheavals which it lacked either the knowledge or the power to master or even to control. Pius IX was the only one who escaped this failure, and he inaugurated the age of the great modern pontiffs, who, with Leo XIII, St Pius X, Pius XI and Pius XII, once more made the Church the sovereign arbitrator of human destiny.

The outstanding worth of the action which the saints exercise on the world lies in its permanence: these men and women of God, who dominated their periods, and captivated their contemporaries by their virtues or their genius, continue, long after their death, to play their exceptional rôles as inspirers and as spiritual guides, are well worth listening to and worthy of being followed. The blood of St Blandina, the thought of St Augustine, the asceticism of St Bernard, and his presence in the world, the humility of St Francis of Assisi, the conquering spirits of St Dominic and of St Francis Xavier, the effective mysticism of St Teresa of Avila, and the discipline of St Ignatius have produced, right up to our own days, and will go on producing, for the service of the Church, generations of martyrs, theologians, ascetics, and apostles, whom the Church will always need in order to carry out her divine mission.

Thus, as those perils, from the proud absolutism of Louis XIV to the intellectual perversion of Karl Marx, against which a weakened papacy found it impossible to oppose a sufficient counterblast, continued to arise, the saints also continued to do battle: there was the radiant spirituality of Francis de Sales, who inaugurated Christian humanism, to which nothing human is foreign since it recognizes a brother, as well as the image of God, in every man; there was the devouring charity of Vincent de Paul, of whom Abbé Bremond said, in a profound passage already quoted, that "it was not his charity which made him a saint, but his sanctity which made him truly charitable" —so important is it not to confuse cause and effect in this matter; there was Monsieur Vincent's sublime love for unhappy mankind, based on the sublimity of his love for God, and there was his desire to live in Christ, to want nothing but what God wanted, to empty himself and to allow God to act; there was the overflowing activity of John Eudes, who broke heroically with the Oratory in order better to be able to arrange his activity, which was destined to provide the Church of the seventeenth century with what she lacked most, priests who were saintly and not merely talented; there was the burning eloquence of Francis Regis, a Jesuit of Cevennes, who captivated the crowds and was a friend to the poor, whom he fed with his own hands and warmed with his smile; there was the triumphant daring of Louis Marie Grignion de Montfort, as pure as an angel and as ready to fight as any knight, who was quick to take out his discipline in order to correct the hooligans of his day, and who dared to cross the threshold of brothels in order to tear the prostitutes from their sin and to help them save their souls; there was the obstinate perseverance of John Baptist de la Salle, an innovator, not understood at first, whose work in education succeeded in raising up, in a society in which faith was wavering, generations of militant Christians who had been formed as children in his school; there was the poignant heroism of Isaac Jogues and John de Brébeuf, missionaries in Canada, who were killed by the Iroquois with refined brutality, martyrs whose generous blood fertilized Canada, where the cross which their mutilated hands had planted has gone on bearing branches, flowers and fruit of evangelical vigour and savour; there was the sublime lice-ridden filth of Benedict Labre who, athirst for God, was determined to have nothing, and to be nothing, but filth—an outcast, a prey to vermin, an eternal wanderer, a beggar and a tramp, the executioner of his own body, spurned, humiliated, despised, insulted, crucified, a challenge to his century of pride and sensuality, to the arrogant, corrupt and sacrilegious eighteenth century, which he loved in spite of everything, to the point of bearing all this in order to draw it, if he could, from all its filth and damnation; there was the moving immolation of Paul of the Cross, in this same age when refinement and bestiality, revolt and abandonment went hand in hand, an immolation which was not a mock torture. In order to bring home to his audience what Christ suffered in his Passion, Paul scourged himself in public until he drew blood; it was an immolation which was also a joy, and an ecstasy in the mystical union with that Jesus for whose sake it was well worth undergoing his martyrdom solely in order to share in his glory even here on earth; there was the startling conversion of Alphonsus de Liguori, the son of the captain-general of the galleys of the King of Naples, who separated from his own proud caste, in order to become the apostle of the humblest people, an advocate solely pleading the cause of God, a fruitful theologian, a keen controversialist and a Christian philosopher who stood up to the atheistic philosophy of his century of false light and eclipsed it; there was the miraculous vocation of Jean-Marie Vianney, a peasant of Dombes, who took hardly to Latin, and yet was more intelligent than any doctor of the university, an obscure priest whose vocation it was one day to become the light of the priesthood, and whose field of action, for forty years, was a village, and, in this tiny village of Ars, an even tinier confessional: he was an insignificant priest whose sanctity radiated from the little village of Ars and lit up the whole Church, bringing light to men who had only just escaped from the bloody abyss of the Revolution; there was the supernatural action undertaken by Don Bosco to win, and preserve for God, the most precious good which the Church has in her care—the abandoned children who are to form the Church's shock troops, the working children among whom the working class must find the apostles it needs to tear them from Marxism which destroys their souls: it was in this, the great struggle of our time, that Don Bosco triumphed, replying, when Christ asked him: "What do you want me to give you?" with the age-old prayer of the saints: "Souls, Lord!"

Souls? In her enclosed Carmel of Lisieux, Teresa of the Child Jesus, a little consumptive immolated by love, with whom the childhood of the Church flowers for ever instead of dying, and Charles de Foucauld, a hermit in the desert which he irrigated with his blood, and whose statue, one must think, will also one day shine in the golden glory of Bernini, surely never wanted anything else from God.

They, like all those who had gone before them, and like all those who will follow in their footsteps, were not of the Church but were the Church. Indeed, the Church acts through her saints, for the Church is her saints. The true history of the Church, as it has rightly been said, is the history of holiness.

SELECT BIBLIOGRAPHY

In this series: COGNET, Louis: *Post-Reformation Spirituality*; CRISTIANI, Léon: *The Revolt Against the Church*; DOUILLET, Jacques: *What is a Saint?*; GUILLEMAIN, Bernard: *The Early Middle Ages; The Later Middle Ages*; PALANQUE, Jean-Rémy: *The Church and the Dark Ages*; ZEILLER, Jacques: *Christian Beginnings*.

ATTWATER, D.: *Martyrs: from St Stephen to John Tung*, London and New York, Sheed and Ward, 1957.

AUCLAIR, Marcelle: *Saint Teresa of Avila*, London, Burns and Oates, and New York, Pantheon, 1953.

BRODRICK, James, S.J.: *St Ignatius Loyola: The Pilgrim Years*, London, Burns and Oates, and New York, Farrar Strauss, 1956; *Origin of the Jesuits*, London and New York, Longmans, 1940; *Progress of the Jesuits*, London and New York, Longmans, 1947; *Saint Francis Xavier*, London, Burns and Oates, and New York, Farrar Strauss, 1952.

BRUNO DE JÉSUS-MARIE, O.C.D.: *St John of the Cross*, London and New York, Sheed and Ward, 1936.

Butler's Lives of the Saints (edited, revised and supplemented by Herbert Thurston, S.J., and Donald Attwater), four volumes, London, Burns and Oates, and New York, Kenedy, 1956. Each entry is followed by a useful bibliography.

CALVET, J.: *Saint Vincent de Paul*, translated by Lancelot C. Sheppard, London, Burns and Oates, and New York, McKay, 1952.

CHALLONER, Richard: *Memoirs of Missionary Priests*, first published London, 1741. The standard modern edition of this classic is that by J. H. Pollen, S.J., London, Burns and Oates, 1924.

CHAMBERS, R. W.: *Thomas More*, London, Cape, 1935, and Westminster, Md, Newman Press, 1949.

COULSON, John (Editor): *The Saints*, London, Burns and Oates, and New York, Hawthorn, 1958.

CURTAYNE, Alice: *Saint Catherine of Siena*, London, Sheed and Ward, 1929.

CUTHBERT of Brighton, Fr, O.F.M. Cap.: *Saint Francis of Assisi*, London, Longmans, 1912; new edn, New York, 1948.

DAWES, Elizabeth, and BAYNES, Norman H.: *Three Byzantine Saints*, Oxford, Blackwell, 1948.

DUDDEN, F. H.: *Life and Times of Saint Ambrose*, two volumes, Oxford, University Press, 1935.

IGNATIUS OF LOYOLA, St: *Spiritual Exercises*, translated by Louis J. Puhl, Westminster, Md, Newman Press, 1951; *Text of the Spiritual Exercises*, translated from the original Spanish, London, Burns and Oates, 1929.

JOHN OF THE CROSS, St: *The Complete Works of St John of the Cross*, translated and edited by E. Allison Peers from the Critical Edition of P. Silverio de Santa Teresa, C.D., three volumes, London, Burns and Oates, and Westminster, Md, Newman Press, 1953.

LAVELLE, Louis: *The Meaning of Holiness* (translated from the French by Dorothea O'Sullivan, with an introduction by Dom Illtyd Trethowan), London, Burns and Oates, 1954, and New York, Pantheon.

SHEPPARD, Lancelot C.: *Barbe Acarie, Wife and Mystic*, London, Burns and Oates, and New York, McKay, 1953; *Portrait of a Parish Priest*, London, Burns and Oates, and Westminster, Md, Newman Press, 1958; *Don Bosco*, London, Burns and Oates, and Westminster, Md, Newman Press, 1957.

TERESA OF JESUS, St: *The Letters of St Teresa of Jesus*, translated and edited by E. Allison Peers from the Critical Edition of P. Silverio de Santa Teresa, C.D., three volumes, London, Burns and Oates, 1951, and Westminster, Md, Newman Press, 1952; *The Complete Works of St Teresa of Jesus*, edited and translated by E. Allison Peers, London and New York, Sheed and Ward, 1946.